Bestselling books k

Speed Writing
Modern Shorthand
UK 9781537566603
World
9781532704918

How to Take Minutes
of Meetings
UK 9781539370376
World
9781532737602

Successful Business
Writing
UK 9781539381839
World
9781532737688

Bestselling books from UoLearn

How to Write
Excellent Reports
UK 9781539381891
World
9781849370899

Developing Your
Assertiveness
UK 9781539391555
World
9781537637723

Developing Your
Influencing Skills
Uk 9781539391517
World
9781537637785

Order books from Amazon or your favourite
bookseller and from www.uolearn.com

Speed Writing Dictionary
Over 7700 Words
An Alternative to Shorthand

Speedwriting dictionary from the BakerWrite system a modern alternative to shorthand including all the 4000 most common words in English.
UK spelling edition.

Published by: Universe of Learning Ltd, reg number 6485477, Lancashire, UK, www.UoLearn.com, support@UoLearn.com

Copyright © 2016
by Joanna Gutmann, Heather Baker and Margaret Greenhall

The moral right of these authors has been asserted.
First Published 2016

ISBN: 978-1537567396

All rights reserved. No part of this book may be reproduced either electronically or on paper without permission in writing from the publisher, except for passages of less than 500 words for purposes of review.

Universe of Learning and UoLearn are trademarks of Universe of Learning Ltd.
BakerWrite is a trademark of Baker Thompson Associates Ltd and is used with permission.

Edited by Dr Margaret Greenhall.

The publisher and author assume no liability for any loss or damage, personal or otherwise which is directly or indirectly caused by the application of any of the contents of this book.

Speed writing dictionary
UK spelling edition

This extended dictionary is the work of three authors.
The BakerWrite speed writing system was created by Heather Baker as an easy to learn alternative to shorthand.
She produced a short dictionary to go along with the course and Joanna Gutmann, a licensed BakerWrite trainer, expanded this to several thousand words. Margaret Greenhall then added to this dictionary and edited it.

This book includes all 4000 of the most common words in written English and lots of business, educational and medical terms.

The BakerWrite system is explained in the companion volume by Heather Baker:

Speed Writing Modern Shorthand
An Easy to Learn Note Taking System,
Heather Baker
ISBN: 978-1537566603
3rd Edition

This is available from Amazon.

This book is intended for you to use interactively.
Please add your own variations as the idea is that it is a reference unique to you. So please feel free to write in the book, that's what the lines are for on each page and the spare pages at the back of the book.
We've worked hard to put in a massive number of words and if you have any suggestions for extra words please let us know and we can add them into the next edition.

If you need any help customer support is available via email support@uolearn.com, weekdays, UK time.

The Authors

Heather Baker

Heather had over twenty years' experience as a secretary and PA before setting up Baker Thompson Associates Limited in 2000. The company specialises in the training and development of PAs and administrative staff, www.bakerthompsonassoc.co.uk.
She is an acclaimed international speaker and has worked in a wide variety of places including London, Liverpool, Paris, Abu Dhabi, Dubai, Singapore, Melbourne, Sydney and Johannesburg. She is a best-selling author of books on speed writing, minute taking and business writing.
Heather worked for ICI Pharmaceuticals (now AstraZeneca) and Hewlett Packard. She spent 5 years in France working for the Commercial Director of Cognac Hine and then 10 years with Granada Media working up to Personal Assistant to the Managing Director, commuting regularly between their offices in Manchester and London.
She created this speed writing system based on some of the principles of shorthand to fulfil a requirement by many companies for a quick and easy way for their employees to take notes. Her speedwriting book is an international best seller.

Joanna Gutmann

Joanna became involved in training whilst working in a PA role in a training centre during the development of a major training program in office and customer-focused communication skills. She left to start her business in the early nineties and continued to work in that area, increasingly specialising in business writing , www.joanna-gutmann.co.uk
Some 15 years ago, inquiries about minute taking increased noticeably which led Joanna to research the area in detail. Having taken minutes for years, she developed a one day

program which gives both the knowledge and the skill to work effectively as a minute taker and that led to her writing the highly successful, 'Taking Minutes of Meetings' (Kogan Page). Today, her business is focused on 'the meeting' with training on chairing, report writing and speed reading

Joanna is delighted to hold a license to run the BakerWrite speed writing training and has found it an invaluable complement to both minute taking and speed reading training. Joanna is also the author of See Me (Blue Ocean) which helps people present the impression of confidence and competence at work and pocket-sized books on punctuation and professional layout.

Margaret Greenhall

Margaret was a chemistry lecturer for eight years and it was during this time that she was asked to teach the foundation study skills to the new students. This started her interest in how people learn and how the learning environment can help them learn better. She moved to staff development and again learned more about how people share information with each other.

In 2003 Margaret left the university to start a training business, www.inspirachange.co.uk specialising in helping people to understand and share information easily and efficiently. This includes topics such as speed reading, improve your memory, creative problem solving and report writing.

She is the best-selling author of Report Writing Skills, (978-1849370899) and combines face to face training with a portfolio of writing and publishing.

a	a	academic	acdmc
abandon	abndn	accelerate	aclrt / acel
abandonment	abndn^m	accent	acnt
abate	abt	accept	acpt
abdomen	abdmn	acceptable	acpt^b
abduct	abdct	acceptance	acpt^c
abduction	abdc^n	access	acs
aberration	abr^n	accessible	acs^b
abeyance	aby^c	accident	acdnt
ability	a^{bty}	accidental	acdntl
able	b	accommodate	^{ac}dt
abolish	abl$_s$	accommodation	^{ac}dt^n
abolition	abl^n	accompany	^{ac}pny
abomination	abmn^n	accomplish	^{ac}pl$_s$
abortion	abr^n	accomplishment	^{ac}pl$_s$^{m}
about	abt	accord	acrd
above	abv	according	acrd^g
abrasion	abr^n	account	acnt
abroad	abrd	accountability	acnt^{bty}
abscond	abscnd	accountable	acnt^b
absconded	abscndd	accountant	acntnt
absence	abs^c	accounting	acnt^g
absolute	abslt	accrue	acru
absolutely	abslt^y	accuracy	acrcy
absorb	absrb	accurate	acrt
absorption	absrp^n	accurately	acrt^y
abstinence	abstn^c	accusation	acus^n
abstract	abstrct	accuse	acus
abundance	abnd^c	achievable	a$_c$v^b
abuse	abus	achieve	a$_c$v
academia	acdma	achieved	a$_c$vd
		achievement	a$_c$v^m
		acid	acd
		acknowledge	aknlj
		acknowledged	aknljd

acne	acn	adjacent	ajcnt
acquire	aqir	adjoining	ajn^g
acquisition	aqs^n	adjourn	ajrn
acquit	aqt	adjournment	ajrn^m
acquitted	aqtd	adjust	ajst
across	acrs	adjustable	ajst^b
act	act	adjustment	ajst^m
action	ac^n	administer	admnstr/ +mnstr
activate	actvt		
activation	actv^n	administration	admnstr^n / adm/+mnstr^n
active	actv		
actively	actv^y	administrative	admnstrtv / +mnstrtv
activist	actvst		
activity	actvy	administrator	admnsttr/ +mnsttr
actor	actr		
actress	actrs	admiration	admr^n/+mr^n
actual	actl	admire	admr / +mr
actually	act^y	admissible	adms^b/+ms^b
acute	acut	admission	adm^n / +m^n
ad	+	admit	admt / +mt
adapt	adpt / +pt	admittance	admt^c / +mt^c
adaptable	adpt^b / +pt^b	adolescence	adls^c / +ls^c
adaptation	adpt^n / +pt^n	adolescent	adlsnt / +lsnt
adaption	adp^n / +p^n	adopt	adpt / +pt
add	+ / ad	adoption	adp^n / +p^n
added	+d	adorable	adr^b / +r^b
addict	adct / +ct	adoration	adr^n / +r^n
addiction	adct^n / +ct^n	adore	adr / +r
addition	ad^n / +t^n	adrenal	adnrl / +nrl
additional	ad^{nl} / +t^{nl}	adult	adlt / +lt
address	adrs / +rs	advance	adv^c / +v^c
adept	adpt / +pt	advanced	adv^{c}d / +v^{c}d
adequate	adqt / +qt	advancement	adv^{cm} / +v^{cm}
adequately	adqt^y / +qt^y	advantage	advntg/+vntg
adherence	adhr^c / +hr^c	advantageous	advntagos / +vntagos
adhesion	adh^n / +h^n		

advent	advnt / +vnt	again	agn
adventure	advntr / +vntr	against	agnst
adverse	advrs / +vrs	age	ag / aj
advert	advrt / +vrt	agency	ag^{cy}
advertise	advrts / +vrts	agenda	agnda / agn
advertisement	advrts^m/+/ad	agent	agnt
advertising	advrts^g/+vrts^g	aggression	agr^n
advice	advc / +vc	aggressive	agrsv
advisable	advs^b / +vs^b	ago	ago
advise	advs / +vs	agonise	agnis
advised	advsd / +vsd	agony	agny
adviser	advsr / +vsr	agree	agre
advisory	advs^y / +vs^y	agreeable	agre^b
advocate	advct / +vct	agreed	agrd
aesthetic	a$_t$tc	agreement	agr^m
affable	af^b	agricultural	agrcltrl
affair	afr	agriculture	agrcltr / agri
affect	afct	ah	ah
affectation	afct^n	ahead	ahd
affection	afc^n	aid	ad
affiliate	aflit	aide	ad
affiliation	afli^n	AIDS	ads
affirm	afrm	ailment	al^m
affirmation	afrm^n	aim	am
affliction	aflc^n	air	ar
affluence	aflu^c	aircraft	arcrft
afford	afrd	airline	arln
affordability	afrd^{bty}	airplane	arpln / pln
affordable	afrd^b	airport	arprt
afraid	afrd	airway	arwy
African	afrcn	aisle	asl
African-American	afrcn-am	alarm	alrm
after	aftr	album	albm
afternoon	aftrnn / pm	alcohol	alchl
afterward	aftrwrd	alcoholism	alchlsm
		alert	alrt

8

alien	alin	altogether	altg$_t$r
alienation	alin^n	aluminium	almnm / al
align	alin	always	alws
alignment	alin^m	AM	am
alike	alk	am	am
alive	alv	amass	ams
all	al	amaze	amz
allegation	alg^n	amazement	amz^m
alleged	algd	amazing	amz^g
allegedly	algd^y	ambassador	ambsdr
allegiance	alegi^c	ambiance	amb^c
allergen	alrgn	ambition	amb^n
allergy	alrgy	ambitious	ambtos
alleviate	aleviat	ambulance	ambl^c
alley	aly / a^y	ambush	amb$_s$
alliance	ali^c	amend	amnd
allocate	alct	amended	amndd
allocated	alctd	amendment	amnd^m
allocation	alc^n	American	amrcn / am
allot	alt	amicable	amc^b
allotment	alt^m	amid	amd
allow	alw	among	amng
allowance	alw^c	amount	amnt
allusion	alu^n	amplify	amplfy
ally	aly / a^y	amputate	amptt
almost	almst	amputated	ampttd
alone	aln	amputation	ampt^n
along	alng	amuse	amus
alongside	alngsd	amusement	amus^m
already	alrdy	an	a
also	als	anaemia	anma
alter	altr	anaesthetic	ans$_t$tc
alteration	altr^n	anaesthetist	ans$_t$tst
altercation	altrc^n	analgesia	anlgsa
alternative	altrntv	analysis	anlyss
although	al$_t$o	analyst	anlyst

analyse	anlys	anybody	nybdy
analysed	anlysd	anymore	nymr
anatomy	antmy	anyone	nyon / an1
ancestor	anstr	anything	ny$_t$^{g}
ancient	ancnt	anyway	nywy
and	&	anywhere	ny$_w$r
and/or	&/r	apart	aprt
and so on	etc	apartment	aprt^m
angel	angl	apologies	aplgs
anger	angr	apologise	aplgis
angle	angl	apology	ap^o
angry	ang^y	apparent	aprnt
animal	anml	apparently	aprnt^y
animation	anm^n	appeal	apel
ankle	ankl	appear	apr
anniversary	anvrs^y / ani	appearance	apr^c
announce	an^c	append	apnd
announcement	an^{cm}	apple	apl
annoy	anoy	appliance	apli^c
annoyance	anoy^c	applicant	aplcnt
annual	anul	application	aplc^n
annually	anu^y	apply	ap^y
annul	anl	appoint	apnt
anonymous	anyms/anom	appointed	apntd
another	ano$_t$r	appointment	apnt^m
answer	ansr	apportion	apr^n
answerable	ansr^b	appraisal	aprsl
anteater	antetr	appraise	aprs
antelope	antlp	appreciable	a^{p}ci^b
antibiotic	antbotc	appreciate	a^{p}cit
anticipate	antcpt	appreciation	a^{p}ci^n
antismoking	antsmk^g	apprehensive	a^{p}nsv
antisocial	ants^s	apprentice	a^{p}ntc
anxiety	anxty	approach	a^p$_c$
anxious	anxs	appropriate	a^{p}rt
any	ny		

approval	a^{p}vl	artery	art^y
approve	a^{p}v	arthritis	a$_t$rits
approved	a^{p}vd	article	artcl
approximate	aprxmt/aprox	articulate	artclt
approximately	aprxmt^y	artificial	artf^s
	aprox^y	artisan	artsn
April	ap	artist	artst
aptitude	aptd / apt	artistic	artstc
Arab	arb	as	as
arbitration	arbtr^n	ash	a$_s$
arch	ar$_c$	Asian	asn / a^n
architect	ar$_c$tct	aside	asd
architecture	ar$_c$tctr	ask	ask
archive	ar$_c$v	asleep	aslp
are	r	aspect	aspct
area	ara	Aspergers	asprgrs
arena	arna	ass	as
arguable	argu^b	assault	aslt
argue	argu	assemble	asmbl
argument	argu^m	assembly	asmb^y
arise	aris	assert	asrt
arm	arm	assertion	asr^n
armed	armd	assertive	asrtv
army	army	assess	ass
around	arnd	assessment	ass^m
arrange	arng / arnj	assessor	assr
arrangement	arng^m	asset	ast
array	ary	assign	asin
arrest	arst	assignation	asgn^n
arrival	arvl	assignment	asin^m
arrive	arv	assist	asst
arrogance	arog^c	assistance	asst^c
arrogant	arognt	assistant	astnt
arrow	arw	associate	asocit
art	art	associated	asocitd
artefact	artfct	association	asoci^n

11

assorted	asrtd	audible	aud^b
assortment	asrt^m	audience	audi^c
assume	asum	audio conference	aud^{c}fr^c
assumption	asmp^n	audit	audt
assurance	asr^c	audition	aud^n
assure	a$_s$r	August	au
assured	a$_s$rd	aunt	ant
astonish	astn$_s$	authentic	au$_t$ntc
astound	astnd	authenticate	au$_t$nct
astronomer	astrnmr	author	au$_t$r
astronomy	astrnmy	authorisation	au$_t$rs^n
at	@	authorise	au$_t$rs
athlete	a$_t$lt	authority	au$_t$rty
athletic	a$_t$ltc	autism	autsm
atmosphere	atmsfr/atmos	autistic	autstc
atom	atm	auto	auto
atop	atp	automatic	automtc
attach	at$_c$	automatically	automtc^y
attachment	at$_c$^{m}	automobile	autombl/auto
attack	atk	autonomy	autonmy
attacked	atkd	autumn	atmn
attain	atn	availability	avl^{bty}
attainable	atn^b	available	avl^b
attainment	atn^m	average	avrj / ave
attempt	atmpt	aversion	avr^n
attend	atnd	avoid	avd
attendance	atnd^c	avoidable	avd^b
attendee	atnde	avoidance	avd^c
attention	atn^n	await	awt
attitude	atitd	awake	awk
attorney	atrny	award	awrd
attract	atrct	aware	awr
attraction	atrc^n	awareness	awrns
attractive	atrcv	away	awy
attribute	atrbt / atrib	awful	aw^f
auction	auc^n		

B

baby	bby / bb
bachelor	b_clr
back	bk
backdate	bkdt
backdated	bkdtd
background	bkgrnd
backup	bkup
backyard	bkyrd
bacteria	bctra
bad	bd
badly	bd^y
baffle	bfl
bag	bg
baguette	bget
bake	bk / bak
balance	bl^c
balanced	bl^{c}d
ball	bl
balloon	blon
ballot	blt
ban	bn
banana	bnna
band	bnd
banish	bn_s
bank	bnk
banker	bnkr
banking	bnk^g
bankrupt	bnkrpt
bankruptcy	bnkrptc
bankrupted	bnkrptd
banquet	bnqt
bar	br
bare	br / bar
barely	br^y
bargain	brgn
barn	brn
barrel	brl
barrier	brr
barrister	brstr
base	bs
baseball	bsbl
basement	bs^m
bashful	b_s^f
basic	bsc
basically	bsc^y
basis	bss
basket	bskt
basketball	bsktbl
bat	bt
batch	b_c
bath	b_t
bathroom	b_trm
battery	bt^y
battle	btl
be	b
beach	b_c
beam	bm
bean	bn
bear	br
bearable	br^b
beard	brd
beast	bst
beat	bt
beautiful	bti^f
beauty	bty
because	bcas

13

beckon	bkn	benevolent	bnvlnt
become	bcm	bereaved	brevd
bed	bd	bereavement	brev^m
bedroom	bdrm	beside	bsd
bee	be	besides	bsds
beef	bf	bespoke	bspk
been	b	best	bst
beer	br	bet	bt
before	bfr / b4	better	btr
befriend	bfrnd	between	btwn
beg	bg	bewildered	bwldrd
began	bgn	bewildering	bwldr^g
begin	bgn	beyond	bynd
beginning	bgn^g	bias	bs
behalf	bhlf	Bible	b^b
behave	bhv	bicycle	bcycl / bike
behaviour	bhvr	bid	bd
behavioural	bhvrl	bidder	bdr
behind	bhnd	big	bg
being	b	bike	bk / bik
belief	blf	bill	bl
believable	blv^b	billion	bln / 10^9
believe	blv	bind	bind / bnd
bell	bl	binge	bng / bnj
belly	b^y	biography	bgrfy / b^o
belong	blng	biological	b^{o}cl
below	blw / blo	biology	b^o
belt	blt	bioscience	biosi^c
bemused	bmsd	birch	br$_c$
bench	bn$_c$	bird	brd
bend	bnd	birth	br$_t$
beneath	bn$_t$	birthday	br$_t$dy
beneficial	bnf^s	bishop	b$_s$p
benefit	bnft	bit	bt
benevolence	bnvl^c	bite	bit
		bitter	btr

black	blk	bomb	bmb
bladder	bldr	bombing	bmb^g
blade	bld	bond	bnd
blame	blm	bone	bn
blank	blnk	bone marrow	bnmrw
blanket	blnkt	bonus	bns
blast	blst	book	bk
blaze	blz	bookkeeper	bkkpr
bleed	bled	bookkeeping	bkkp^g
blemish	blm_s	boom	bm / bom
blend	blnd	boost	bst
bless	bls	boot	bt / bot
blessing	bls^g	booth	b_t / bo_t
blind	blnd	border	brdr
blink	blnk	bordered	brdrd
block	blk	bore	br
blog	blg	boring	br^g
blond	blnd	born	brn
blood	bld	borrow	brw
bloody	bldy	boss	bs
blossom	blsm	botany	btny
blotch	bl_c	both	b_t
blow	blw	bother	b_t r
blue	blu	bottle	btl
bluff	blf	bottom	btm
blunder	blndr	bought	bt
blur	blr	bounce	bo^c
blurt	blrt	bound	bnd / bond
blush	bl_s	boundary	bnd^y
board	brd	bow	bw / bo
boast	bost	bowel	bwl
boat	bt	bowl	bwl
body	bdy	box	bx
boil	bol	boy	by
bold	bld	boycott	byct
bolt	blt	boyfriend	byfrnd

15

brain	brn	broke	brk
brake	brk	broken	brkn
branch	brn_c	broker	brkr
brand	brnd	bronze	brnz
brave	brv	brother	br_t r
bread	brd	brought	brt
break	brk	brown	brn
breakable	brk^b	brown field	brnfld
breakdown	brkdn	brush	br_s
breakfast	brkfst	brutal	brtl
breakthrough	brk_t ru	brutalised	brtlsd
breast	brst	bubble	bbl
breath	br_t	buck	bk
breathable	br_t^b	bucket	bkt
breathe	br_t e	Buddhist	bdst
breathing	br_t^g	buddy	bdy
breeze	brz	budget	bdgt
brick	brk	buffalo	bflo
bricklayer	brklyr	bug	bg
bridal	brdl	build	bld
bride	brd / brid	builder	bldr
bridesmaid	brdsmd	building	bld^g
bridge	brg / brj	bulb	blb
brief	brf	bulk	blk
briefly	brf^y	bull	bl
bright	brt	bullet	blt
brilliance	brli^c	bulletin	bltn
brilliant	brlint / bril	bullied	bld
bring	br^g	bully	b^y
bringing	br^gg	bunch	bn_c
British	brt_s / brit	bungalow	bnglw
broach	br_c	bungle	bngl
broad	brd	buoyant	bynt
broadcast	brdcst	burden	brdn
brochure	br_s r	bureau	bru
		burn	brn

16

burning	brn^g		
bury	b^y		
bus	bs		
bush	b$_s$		
business	bsns / bs		
businessman	bsnsmn		
businesswoman	bsnswmn		
busy	bsy		
but	bt		
butcher	bt$_c$r		
butt	bt		
butter	btr		
butterfly	btrf^y		
button	btn		
buy	by / bi		
buyer	byr / bir		
by	by / bi		

C

cab	cb
cabin	cbn
cabinet	cbnt
cable	c^b
cage	cg / cj
cake	ck
calculate	clcult / calc
calculation	clcul^n
calendar	clndr / cal
calibrate	clbrt
calibration	clbr^n
call	cl
caller	clr
calliper	clpr
calm	clm
calories	clrs / cals
came	cm
camera	cmra
camp	cmp
campaign	cmpn
campus	cmps
can	cn / k
can't	cnt
Canadian	cndn / ca
cancel	cncl / kncl
cancellation	cncl^n
cancelled	cncld
cancer	cncr / kncr
candidate	cndt
candle	cndl
candy	cndy

17

canvas	cnvs	cart	crt
canvass	cnvs	cartilage	crtlg / crtlj
cap	cp	cartoon	crtn
capability	cp^{bty}	carve	crv
capable	cp^b	carwash	crw$_s$
capacity	cpcty	cascade	cscd
capital	cptl	case	cs
capitalise	cptlis	cash	c$_s$
capped	cpd	cashier	c$_s$ier
capsule	cpsul	casino	csno
captain	cptn	cast	cst
caption	cp^n	castigated	cstgtd
captivated	cptvtd	castigation	cstg^n
captivating	cptvt^g	casual	csul
captive	cptv	casualty	csulty
capture	cptr	cat	ct
car	cr	catalogue	ctalg
carbohydrate	crbhydrt/carb	catch	c$_c$
carbon	crbn	catchment	c$_c$^{m}
carbonation	crbn^n	category	ctg^y / cat
card	crd	cater	ctr
cardiac	crdac	caterpillar	ctrplr
cardio	crdio	cathedral	c$_t$drl
cardiologist	crdiolgst	catheter	c$_t$tr
care	car	Catholic	c$_t$olc / cath
career	crr	cattle	ctl
careful	car^f	caught	ct
carefully	car^{fy}	causation	csa^n
carer	carr	cause	cs
caretaker	cartkr	causes	css
cargo	crgo	caution	c^n
carpenter	crpntr	cave	cv
carpet	crpt	cavity	cvty
carrier	crr	cease	ces
carrot	crt	ceiling	cl^g
carry	c^y	celebrate	clbrt

celebration	clbr^n	channel	$_c$nl
celebrity	clbrty	chaos	$_c$s / kos
cell	cl / sl	chaplain	$_c$pln
cemetery	cmt^y	chapter	$_c$ptr
censor	cnsr	character	$_c$rctr
censorship	cnsr^p	characterise	$_c$rctrs
censure	cnsr	characteristic	$_c$rctrstc
censured	cnsrd	charge	$_c$rg
cent	cnt	chargeable	$_c$rg^b
centipede	cntpd	charitable	$_c$rt^b
central	cntrl	charity	$_c$rty
centre	cntr	charm	$_c$rm
century	cnt^y	chart	$_c$rt
CEO	ceo	charter	$_c$rtr
ceremony	crmny	chartered	$_c$rtrd
certain	crtn	chase	$_c$s
certifiable	crtfi^b	chasten	$_c$sn
certificate	crtfct / cert	chat	$_c$t
certify	crtfy	cheap	$_c$p
cervical	crvcl	cheat	$_c$t
cessation	cs^n	check	$_c$k
chain	$_c$n	cheek	$_c$k / $_c$ek
chainsaw	$_c$nsw	cheer	$_c$r
chair	$_c$r	cheese	$_c$es
chairman	$_c$rmn	chef	$_c$f
chairperson	$_c$rprsn	chemical	$_c$mcl
chairwoman	$_c$rwmn	chemistry	$_c$mst^y / chem
challenge	$_c$lng	chemotherapy	$_c$mo$_t$rpy/chemo
chamber	$_c$mbr	chest	$_c$st
champion	$_c$mpin/champ	chew	$_c$w
championship	$_c$mpin^p	chick	$_c$k
chance	$_c$n^c	chicken	$_c$kn
change	$_c$ng	chief	$_c$f
changeable	$_c$ng^b	child	$_c$ld
changing	$_c$ng^g	childhood	$_c$ldhd

19

childminder	c ldmndr	civil	cvl
children	c ldrn	civilian	cvln / civi
chill	c l	civilisation	cvlsa[n]
chimpanzee	c mpnz / c mp	civilise	cvls
chin	c n	claim	clm
Chinese	c ns	clarified	clrfd
chip	c p	clarify	clrfy
chocolate	c clt	clash	cl_s
choice	c c	clasp	clsp
choke	c k	class	cls
cholesterol	c lstrl	classic	clsc
choose	c os	classical	clscl
chop	c p	classification	clsfc[n]
chord	c rd	classify	clsfy
chorus	c rs	classroom	clsrm
chose	c s	clay	cly / cla
Christian	c rs[n]	clean	cln
Christianity	c rs[nty]	cleanse	cl[c]
Christmas	c rsms / xmas	clear	cler
chronic	c rnc / krnc	clearance	cler[c]
chronicle	c rncl / krncl	clearly	cler[y]
chunk	c nk	clerk	clrk
church	c [r]c	click	clk
cigarette	cgrt / cig	client	clnt
circle	crcl	cliff	clf
circuit	crct	climate	clmt
circulate	crclt	climb	clim
circulating	crclt[g]	cling	cl[g]
circulation	crcl[n]	clinging	cl[gg]
circumstance	crcmst[c]	clinic	clnc / klnc
citation	cita[n]	clinical	clncl
cite	ct / st	clip	clp
citizen	ctzn	clock	clk
citizenship	ctzn[p]	clone	cln
city	cty	close	cls
civic	cvc	closed	clsd

closely	cls^y	coin	cn
closer	clsr	coincide	concd
closest	clst	coincidence	concd^c
closet	clset	cold	cld
clot	clt	collaborate	clbrt
cloth	cl_t	collaboration	clbr^n
clothe	clo_t	collapse	clps
clothes	cl_t s	collapsible	clps^b
clothing	cl_t^g	collar	clr
cloud	cld	collate	clt
club	clb	collated	cltd
clue	clu	colleague	cleg
cluster	clstr	collect	clct
clutch	cl_c	collectible	clct^b
coach	c_c	collection	clc^n
coagulate	coaglt / coag	collective	clctv
coagulation	coagl^n/coag^n	collector	cltr
coal	cl	college	clg / clj
coalition	cali^n	collision	cl^n
coast	cst	collusion	clu^n
coastal	cstl	colon	cln
coat	ct	colonial	clnl
co-author	c-au_t r	colony	clny
cocaine	ccan	colour	clr
code	cd	colourful	clr^f
coeducation	coedc^n	column	clm
coeducational	coedc^nl/coed	columnist	clmst
coerce	coerc	coma	^c a
coerced	coercd	comatose	^c atos
coexist	coexst	combat	^c bt
coffee	cfe	combination	^c bna^n
cognition	cgn^n	combine	^c bn
cognitive	cgntv	combined	^c bnd
cohabit	cohbt	combustible	^c bst^b
coherent	cohrnt	combustion	^c bst^n
cohesion	coh^n	come	cm / ^c

21

comeback	cmbk / ᶜbk	commonality	ᶜnlty
comedy	ᶜdy	commonly	ᶜnʸ
comeuppance	cmupᶜ / ᶜupᶜ	commonplace	ᶜnplc
comfort	ᶜfrt	commonsense	ᶜnsᶜ
comfortable	ᶜfrtᵇ	commotion	ᶜmⁿ
comfortably	ᶜfrtᵇʸ	communal	ᶜunl
comforted	ᶜfrtd	communicable	ᶜunicᵇ
comic	ᶜc	communicate	ᶜunict
coming	cmᵍ / ᶜᵍ	communication	ᶜunicⁿ
command	ᶜnd	community	ᶜunty
commanded	ᶜndd	commute	ᶜt
commander	ᶜndr	compact	ᶜpct
commandment	ᶜndᵐ	companion	ᶜpnn
commence	cc	company	ᶜpny
commencement	ccm	comparability	ᶜprᵇᵗʸ
commencing	cg	comparable	ᶜprᵇ
commend	ᶜnd	comparably	ᶜprᵇʸ
commendable	ᶜndᵇ	compare	ᶜpr
comment	cm	comparison	ᶜprsn
commentary	cmy	compartment	ᶜprtᵐ
commented	cmd	compassion	ᶜpⁿ
commenting	cmg	compel	ᶜpl
commerce	ᶜrs	compelled	ᶜpld
commercial	ᶜrˢ	compelling	ᶜplᵍ
commercialise	ᶜrˢis	compensate	ᶜpnst
commercially	ᶜrˢʸ	compensation	ᶜpnsⁿ
commiserate	ᶜsrt	compete	ᶜpt
commission	ᶜiⁿ	competence	ᶜptᶜ
commissioned	ᶜiⁿd	competency	ᶜptᶜʸ
commissioner	ᶜiⁿr	competent	ᶜptnt
commissions	ᶜiⁿs	competition	ᶜptⁿ / comp
commit	ᶜt	competitive	ᶜpttv
commitment	ᶜtᵐ	competitor	ᶜpttr
committee	ᶜte	compilation	ᶜplaⁿ
commodity	ᶜodty	compile	ᶜpl
common	ᶜn	complain	ᶜpln

22

complained	ᶜplnd	computerised	ᶜptrsd
complaint	ᶜplnt	computing	ᶜpt^g
complement	ᶜpl^m	comrade	ᶜrd
complementary	ᶜpl^my	comradeship	ᶜrd^p
complete	ᶜplt	concave	ᶜcv
completed	ᶜpltd	conceal	ᶜcel
completely	ᶜplt^y	concealed	ᶜceld
completion	ᶜpl^n	concede	ᶜced
complex	ᶜplx	conceded	ᶜcedd
complexity	ᶜplxty	conceivable	ᶜcv^b
compliance	ᶜpli^c	conceivably	ᶜcv^by
compliant	ᶜplint	conceive	ᶜcev
complicate	ᶜplct	concentrate	ᶜcntrt
complicated	ᶜplctd	concentrated	ᶜcntrtd/concd
complication	ᶜplc^n	concentration	ᶜcntr^t / conc
complicit	ᶜplst / ᶜplct	concept	ᶜcpt
compliment	ᶜpl^m	conception	ᶜcp^n
complimentary	ᶜpl^my	concepts	ᶜcpts
comply	ᶜp^y	concern	ᶜcrn
component	ᶜpnt	concerned	ᶜcrnd
compose	ᶜps	concerning	ᶜcrn^g
composition	ᶜps^n	concert	ᶜcrt
composure	ᶜpsr	concession	ᶜs^n
compound	ᶜpnd	conciliated	ᶜcliatd
comprehend	ᶜprhnd	conciliation	ᶜclia^n
comprehension	ᶜprhn^n	conciliatory	ᶜcliat^y
comprehensive	ᶜprhnsv	concise	ᶜcs
comprise	ᶜprs	conclude	ᶜcld
comprised	ᶜprsd	concluded	ᶜcldd
compromise	ᶜprms	conclusion	ᶜcl^n
compulsion	ᶜpl^n	conclusive	ᶜclsv
compulsive	ᶜplsv	concoct	ᶜcct
compulsory	ᶜpls^y	concoction	ᶜcc^n
compunction	ᶜpnct^n	concrete	ᶜcrt
computer	ᶜptr	concur	ᶜcr
computerise	ᶜptris	concurred	ᶜcrd

concurrence	^{c}cr^c	confidentially	^{c}fdn^{sy}
concurrent	^{c}crnt	configuration	^{c}fgr^n
concuss	^{c}cs	configure	^{c}fgr
concussion	^{c}cs^n	confine	^{c}fn
condemn	^{c}dm	confined	^{c}fnd
condemned	^{c}dmd	confinement	^{c}fn^m
condense	^{c}d^c	confirm	^{c}frm
condensed	^{c}d^{c}d	confirmation	^{c}frm^n
condescend	^{cd}nd	confirmed	^{c}frmd
condition	^{c}d^n	confiscate	^{c}fsct
conditional	^{c}d^{nl}	conflict	^{c}flct
conditionality	^{c}d^{nl}ty	conform	^{c}frm
conditioned	^{c}d^{n}d	conformed	^{c}frmd
condolence	^{c}dl^c	conforms	^{c}frms
condom	^{c}dm	confound	^{c}fnd
condone	^{c}dn	confounded	^{c}fndd
condoned	^{c}dnd	confront	^{c}frnt
conduct	^{c}dct	confrontation	^{c}frnt^n
conduit	^{c}duit	confrontational	^{c}frnt^{nl}
confection	^{c}fc^n	confuse	^{c}fs
confectionery	^{c}fc^{ny}	confusingly	^{c}fs^{gy}
confederacy	^{c}fdrcy	confusion	^{c}fs^n
confederate	^{c}fdrt	congeal	^{c}gel
confer	^{c}fr	congenial	^{c}gnial
conference	^{c}fr^c	congestion	^{c}gst^n
confess	^{c}fs	conglomerate	^{c}glmrt
confesses	^{c}fss	congratulate	^{c}grtlt
confession	^{c}f^n	congress	^{c}grs
confessional	^{c}fs^{nl}	congressional	^{c}gr^{nl}
confidant	^{c}fdnt	conjecture	^{c}jctur
confide	^{c}fid	conjoined	^{c}jnd
confided	^{c}fdd	conjunction	^{c}jnc^n
confidence	^{c}fd^c	conjure	^{c}jr
confident	^{c}fdnt	connect	^{c}ect
confidential	^{c}fdn^s	connectible	^{c}ect^b
confidentiality	^{c}fdn^{s}lty	connection	^{c}ec^n

connector	ᶜectr	consort	ᶜsrt
conqueror	ᶜqrr	consortium	ᶜsrtim
conquest	ᶜqst	conspicuous	ᶜspcos
conscience	ᶜsᶜ	conspiracy	ᶜsprcy
conscientious	ᶜsnsos	conspire	ᶜspr
conscious	ᶜsos	constable	ᶜstᵇ
consciously	ᶜsosʸ	constabulary	ᶜstblʸ
consciousness	ᶜsosns	constant	ᶜstnt
consecutive	ᶜsctv	constantly	ᶜstntʸ
consecutively	ᶜsctvʸ	constipate	ᶜstpt
consensus	ᶜsnss	constituent	ᶜsttunt
consent	ᶜsnt	constitute	ᶜsttut
consequence	ᶜsqᶜ	constitution	ᶜsttuⁿ
consequential	ᶜsqnˢ	constitutional	ᶜsttuⁿˡ
consequently	ᶜsqntʸ	constrain	ᶜstrn
conservation	ᶜsrvⁿ	constrained	ᶜstrnd
conservative	ᶜsrvtv	constraint	ᶜstrnt
conserve	ᶜsrv	constraints	ᶜstrnts
consider	ᶜsdr	constrict	ᶜstrct
considerable	ᶜsdrᵇ	construct	ᶜstrct
considerably	ᶜsdrᵇʸ	constructed	ᶜstrctd
considerate	ᶜsdrt	construction	ᶜstrctⁿ
consideration	ᶜsdrⁿ	constructive	ᶜstrctv
considered	ᶜsdrd	constructively	ᶜstrctvʸ
considers	ᶜsdrs	constructor	ᶜstrctr
consignment	ᶜsnᵐ	construe	ᶜstru
consignments	ᶜsnᵐs	consular	ᶜsulr
consist	ᶜst	consult	ᶜslt
consistency	ᶜstᶜʸ	consultancy	ᶜsltᶜʸ
consistent	ᶜstnt	consultant	ᶜsltnt
consistently	ᶜstntʸ	consultation	ᶜsltⁿ
consolation	ᶜslⁿ	consulted	ᶜsltd
console	ᶜsl	consumable	ᶜsmᵇ
consolidate	ᶜsldt	consume	ᶜsm
consolidated	ᶜsldtd	consumer	ᶜsmr
consonant	ᶜsnnt	consumerism	ᶜsmrsm

consummate	ᶜsmt	control	ᶜtrl
consummation	ᶜsmaⁿ	controllable	ᶜtrlᵇ
consumption	ᶜsmpⁿ	controls	ᶜtrls
contact	ᶜtct	controversial	ᶜtrvˢ
contagious	ᶜtgos / ᶜtjos	controversy	ᶜtrvsy
contain	ᶜtn	conundrum	ᶜndrm
container	ᶜtnr	conurbation	ᶜrbⁿ
containment	ᶜtnᵐ	convalesce	ᶜvls
contemplate	ᶜtmplt	convalescence	ᶜvlsᶜ
contemporary	ᶜtmpʸ	convalescent	ᶜvlsnt
contempt	ᶜtmpt	convection	ᶜvcⁿ
contemptible	ᶜtmptᵇ	convene	ᶜvn
contend	ᶜtnd	convened	ᶜvnd
content	ᶜtnt	convenience	ᶜvniᶜ
contention	ᶜtnⁿ	convenient	ᶜvnint
contentment	ᶜtntᵐ	convention	ᶜvnⁿ
contest	ᶜtst	conventional	ᶜvnⁿˡ
contested	ᶜtstd	converged	ᶜvrgd
context	ᶜtxt	convergence	ᶜvrgᶜ
continence	ᶜtnᶜ	converging	ᶜvngᵍ
continent	ᶜtnnt	conversant	ᶜvrsnt
contingency	ᶜtngᶜʸ	conversation	ᶜvrsⁿ
continuation	ᶜtnuⁿ	converse	ᶜvrs
continue	ᶜtnu	conversely	ᶜvrsʸ
continued	ᶜtnud	conversion	ᶜvrⁿ
continuing	ᶜtnuᵍ	convert	ᶜvrt
continuous	ᶜtnos	convertible	ᶜvrtᵇ
contract	ᶜtrct	converting	ᶜvrtᵍ
contracted	ᶜtrctd	convex	ᶜvx
contraction	ᶜtrcⁿ	convey	ᶜvy
contractor	ᶜtrctr	conveyance	ᶜvyᶜ
contradiction	ᶜtrdcⁿ	convict	ᶜvct
contrast	ᶜtrst	convicted	ᶜvctd
contribute	ᶜtrbt	conviction	ᶜvcⁿ
contribution	ᶜtrbⁿ	convince	ᶜvᶜ
contributor	ᶜtrbtr	convinced	ᶜvᶜd

convincingly	cvncgy	corrupt	crpt
convoluted	cvltd	corruption	crpn
convolution	cvlun	cost	cst
convulse	cvls	costed	cstd
convulsion	cvln	costly	csty
cook	ck	costume	cstm
cookie	cke	cottage	ctg / ctj
cooking	ckg	cotton	ctn
cool	cl	cough	cf
cooperate	coprt	could	cd
cooperation	coprn	council	cncl
cooperative	coprtv / coop	councillor	cnslr
co-opted	c-ptd	counsel	cnsl
coordinate	cordnt/coor	counselled	cnsld
coordinator	cordntr	counselling	cnslg
cop	cp	counsellor	cnslr
cope	cop	count	cnt
copy	cpy	counter	cntr
copy edit	cpyedt	counterpart	cntrprt
cord	crd	country	cnty
core	cr	county	cnty
corn	crn	coup	co
corner	crnr	couple	cpl
coronary	crny	coupon	copn
coroner	crnr	courage	crg /crj
corporate	crprt	course	crs
corporation	crprn /corp	court	crt
correct	crct	courtroom	crtrm
correction	crcn	cousin	csn
correctly	crcty	covenant	cvnnt
correlate	crlt	cover	cvr
correlation	crlan	coverage	cvrg / cvrj
correspondence	crspndc	covers	cvrs
correspondent	crspndnt	cow	cw
corridor	crdr	crab	crb
corrosion	crn	crack	crk

cracked	crkd	cruel	crul
craft	crft	cruise	crs
crash	cr$_s$	crush	cr$_s$
crave	crv	crutch	cr$_c$
crawl	crwl	cry	c^y
crazy	crzy	crystal	crstl
cream	crem	Cuban	cbn / cu
crease	crs	cue	cu
create	crat	culminate	clmnt
creation	cra^n	culmination	clmn^n
creative	cratv	culpability	clp^{bty}
creativity	cratvy	culpable	clp^b
creature	crtr	cult	clt
crèche	cr$_c$	cultivate	cltvt
credence	crd^c	cultivation	cltv^n
credential	crdn^s	cultural	cltrl
credibility	crd^{bty}	culture	cltr
credible	crd^b	cup	cp
credit	crdt	curate	curt
creditable	crdt^b	curb	crb
cremation	crm^n	cure	cur
crew	crw	curiosity	cristy
crime	crm	curious	cros
criminal	crmnl	currency	cr^{cy}
crisis	crs	current	curnt
criteria	crta	currently	crnt^y
critic	crtc	curriculum	crclm
critical	crtcl	curtain	crtn
criticise	crtcs	curve	crv
criticised	crtcsd	cushion	c$_s$n
criticism	crtsm	custody	cstdy
crocodile	crcdl / croc	custom	cstm
crop	crp	customer	cstmr
cross	crs	cut	ct
crowd	crwd	cute	cut
crowded	crwdd	cycle	ccl
crucial	cr^s		

D

dad	dd
daily	dly / d^y
dam	dm
damage	dmg / dmj
damn	dm
dance	d^c
dancer	d^{c}r
dancing	d^{cg}
danger	dngr
dangerous	dngros
dare	dr
dark	drk
darkness	drkns
dash	d$_s$
data	dta
database	dtabs
date	dt
daughter	dtr
daunt	dnt
dawn	dwn
day	dy
dead	dd
deadline	ddln
deadly	dd^y
deal	dl
dealer	dlr
dealership	dlr^p
dear	dr
death	d$_t$
debate	dbt
debated	dbtd
debrief	dbrf
debris	dbri
debt	dt
debtor	dtr
debunk	dbnk
debut	dbt
decade	dcd
decadence	dcd^c
decay	dcy
decease	dces
deceased	dcesd
deceit	dcet
deceitful	dcet^f
December	de
decent	dcnt
deception	dcp^n
decide	dcd
decided	dcdd
decimal	dcml
decision	dc^n
deck	dk
declaration	dclra^n
declare	dclr
declared	dclrd
decline	dcln
decode	dcod
decompose	dcmps
decorate	dcrt
decoration	dcr^n
decrease	dcres
dedicate	ddct
dedication	ddc^n
deduct	ddct
deductible	ddct^b
deduction	ddc^n
deem	dm
deep	dp
deepen	dpn

29

deeper	dpr	degradation	dgrda^n
deeply	dp^y	degrade	dgrd
deer	dr	degree	dgre
deface	dfc	dehydrate	dhydrt
defamation	dfm^n	dehydration	dhydr^n
defeat	dfet	deject	djct
defeated	dfetd	dejection	djct^n
defect	dfct	delay	dly
defective	dfctv	delayed	dlyd
defence	df^c	delegate	dlgt
defend	dfnd	delegation	dlg^n
defendant	dfndnt	delete	dlet
defender	dfndr	deletion	dl^n
defensive	df^{c}v	deliberate	dlbrt
defer	dfr	deliberately	dlbrt^y
deferential	dfrn^s	deliberation	dlbr^n
deferred	dfrd	delicate	dlct
defiance	dfi^c	delight	dlt
defiant	dfint	delightful	dlt^f
deficiency	dfs^{cy}	delineation	dlnea^n
deficient	dfst	deliver	dlvr
deficit	dfct	deliverable	dlvr^b
define	dfn	deliverance	dlvr^c
defined	dfnd	delivery	dlv^y
defining	dfn^g	delusion	dl^n
definite	dfnt	demand	dmnd
definitely	dfnt^y	demarcate	dmrct
definition	dfn^n	demarcation	dmrc^n
deflate	dflt	demean	dmen
deflation	dfl^n	dementia	d$_m$a
deforestation	dfrst^n	democracy	dmocrcy
deform	dfrm	democrat	dmocrt
deformation	dfrm^n	democratic	dmocrtc
defunct	dfnct	demographic	dmogrfc
defuse	dfus	demolish	dml$_s$
defy	dfy	demolition	dml^n

demonstrate	dmnstrt	deprivation	dprv^n
demonstrated	dmnstrtd	depth	dp$_t$
demonstration	dmnstr^n	deputy	dpty
demotion	dm^n	derelict	drlct
denial	dnl	dereliction	drlc^n
denigrate	dngrt	derivation	drva^n
denigration	dngr^n	derive	driv
dense	d^c	dermatology	drmt^o
density	d^{c}ty	descendant	^{d}ndnt
deny	dny	descended	^{d}ndd
depart	dprt	descends	^{d}nds
departed	dprtd	descent	^{d}nt
department	dprt^m / dpt	describable	^{d}crb^b
departmental	dprt^{ml} / dpt^{ml}	describe	^{d}crb
departure	dpftr	described	^{d}crbd
depend	dpnd / dep	description	^{d}crp^n
dependable	dpnd^b / dep^b	descriptive	^{d}crptv
dependence	dpnd^c / dep^c	desecrate	^{d}scrt
dependency	dpnd^{cy}/dep^{cy}	desecration	^{d}scr^n
dependent	dpndnt/depnt	deselect	^{d}lct
depending	dpnd^g / dep^g	deselected	^{d}lctd
depict	dpct	desert	^{d}rt
depiction	dpct^n	deserted	^{d}rtd
deplete	dplet	deserter	^{d}rtr
depletion	dpl^n	desertion	^{d}r^n
deplorable	dplr^b	deserve	^{d}rv
deplore	dplr	deserved	^{d}rvd
deploy	dply	deservedly	^{d}rvd^y
deployment	dply^m	deserves	^{d}rvs
deport	dprt	design	^{d}n
deportation	dprt^n	designate	^{d}ignt
deposit	dpst	designated	^{d}igntd
depress	dprs	designation	^{d}ign^n
depressant	dprnt	designed	^{d}ind
depressed	dprsd	designer	^{d}inr
depression	dpr^n	desirability	^{d}ir^{bty}

31

desirable	d$_{ir}$b	destructible	d$_{trc}$b
desire	d$_{ir}$	destruction	d$_{trc}$n
desired	d$_{ird}$	destructive	d$_{trctv}$
desist	d$_{st}$	detach	dt$_c$
desisted	d$_{std}$	detached	dt$_c$d
desk	d$_k$	detachment	dt$_c$m
desk bound	d$_{kbnd}$	detail	dtl
desktop	d$_{ktp}$	detailed	dtld
desolate	d$_{olt}$	detain	dtn
desolation	d$_{olt}$n	detect	dtct
despair	d$_{pr}$	detected	dtctd
despaired	d$_{prd}$	detection	dtc^n
despairingly	d$_{pr}$gy	detective	dtctv
desperate	d$_{prt}$	detention	dtn^n
desperately	d$_{prt}$y	deter	dtr
desperation	d$_{pr}$n	determination	dtrmn^n
despicable	d$_{pc}$b	determine	dtrmn
despicably	d$_{pc}$by	determined	dtrmnd
despise	d$_{ps}$	determining	dtrmn^g
despised	d$_{psd}$	deterrence	dtr^c
despite	d$_{pt}$	deterring	dtr^g
despondency	d$_{pnd}$cy	detest	dtst
despondent	d$_{pndnt}$	detox	dtx
dessert	d$_{rt}$	detoxification	dtxfc^n
destabilisation	d$_{tbls}$n	detract	dtrct
destabilise	d$_{tbls}$	detriment	dtr^m
destabilised	d$_{tblsd}$	detrimental	dtr^{ml}
destination	d$_{tn}$n	devaluation	dvlu^n
destined	d$_{tnd}$	devalue	dvlu
destiny	d$_{tny}$	devastate	dvstt
destitute	d$_{ttut}$	devastating	dvstt^g
destitution	d$_{ttu}$n	devastation	dvst^n
destroy	d$_{try}$	develop	dvlp/dv/dev
destroyed	d$_{tryd}$	developer	dvlpr/dvr/devr
destruct	d$_{trct}$	developing	dvlp^g/dv^g/dev^g
destructed	d$_{trctd}$		

development	dvlp^m /dv^m / dev^m	differently	dfrnt^y
developmental	dvlp^{ml} /dv^{ml} / dev^{ml}	difficult	dfclt / dif
		difficulty	dfclty
		diffidence	dfd^c
deviate	dvit	diffident	dfdnt
deviation	dvi^n	diffuse	dfus
device	dvc	dig	dg
devil	dvl	digest	dgst
devolution	dvlu^n	digestion	dgst^n
devolve	dvlv	digital	dgtl
devote	dvt	dignity	dgnty
devotion	dv^n	dilate	dlat
diabetes	diabts	dilation	dla^n
diagnose	diagns	dilemma	dlma
diagnosis	diagnss	diligence	dlg^c
diagram	diagrm / dia	dimension	dmn^n
dial	dil	diminish	dmn$_s$
dialect	dialct	dining	dn^g
dialogue	dialg	dinner	dnr
dialysis	dialss	dinosaur	dnosr / dino
dialysing	dials^g	diplomat	dplomt
diamond	dimnd	diplomatic	dplomtc
diaphragm	diphm/diafrm	direct	drct
diarrhoea	diarea	direction	drc^n
diary	di^y	directly	drct^y
dictate	dctt	director	drctr / dir
dictation	dct^n	directory	drct^y
diction	dc^n	dirt	drt
dictionary	dc^{ny}	dirty	drty
did	dd	disabilities	^{db}ts
die	di	disability	dbty
diet	diet	disable	db
dietician	diet^n	disabled	^{db}d
differ	dfr	disablement	dbm
difference	dfr^c	disables	^{db}s
different	dfrnt		

disadvantage	^{d}advntg / ^{d}advntj	disciplinary	^{d}pln^y
		discipline	^{d}pln
disadvantaged	^{d}advntgd	disciplined	^{d}plnd
disadvantages	^{d}advntgs	disclose	^{d}cls
disaffect	^{d}afct	disclosed	^{d}clsd
disaffected	^{d}afctd	disclosure	^{d}clsr
disaffection	^{d}afc^n	discolour	^{d}clr
disagree	^{d}agre	discoloured	^{d}clrd
disagreeable	^{d}agr^b	discomfort	^{dc}frt
disagreeably	^{d}agr^{by}	disconcerting	^{dc}crt^g
disagreed	^{d}agrd	disconcertingly	^{dc}crt^{gy}
disagreement	^{d}agr^m	disconnect	^{dc}ct
disallow	^{d}alw	disconnected	^{dc}ctd
disappear	^{d}apr	discontent	^{dc}tnt
disappearance	^{d}apr^c	discontented	^{dc}tntd
disappeared	^{d}aprd	discontinue	^{dc}tnu
disappoint	^{d}apnt	discontinued	^{dc}tnud
disappointed	^{d}apntd	discount	^{d}cnt
disappointment	^{d}apnt^m	discountable	^{d}cnt^b
disapproval	^{d}aprvl	discounted	^{d}cntd
disapprove	^{d}aprv	discourage	^{d}crg / ^{d}crj
disapproved	^{d}aprvd	discouragement	^{d}crg^m
disapprovingly	^{d}aprv^{gy}	discourse	^{d}crs
disarray	^{d}ary	discourtesy	^{d}crtsy
disassociate	^{d}ascit	discover	^{d}cvr
disaster	^{d}astr	discoverable	^{d}cvr^b
disband	^{d}bnd	discovered	^{d}cvrd
disbanded	^{d}bndd	discovery	^{d}cv^y
disbelief	^{d}blf	discredit	^{d}crdt
disc	^{d}c / dsc	discredited	^{d}crdtd
discard	^{d}crd	discrepancy	^{d}crp^{cy}
discarded	^{d}crdd	discretion	^{d}cr^n
discern	^{d}rn	discretionary	^{d}cr^{ny}
discernible	^{d}rn^b	discrimination	^{d}crmn^n
discharge	^{d}crg	discuss	^{d}cs
discharged	^{d}crgd	discussed	^{d}csd

discussion	dc^n	disk	dk
disdain	dsdn	dislike	dlk
disease	des	dislikeable	dlk^b
diseased	desd	disliked	dlkd
disengage	d$engg$/d$engj$	dislikes	dlks
disengaged	d$enggd$	dislocate	dlct
disengagement	d$engg^m$	dislocated	dlctd
disentangle	d$entngl$	dislodge	dlg / dlj
disfigure	dfgr	dislodged	dlgd
disfigured	dfgrd	disloyal	dlyl
disfigurement	dfgr^m	disloyalty	dlylty
disgrace	dgrc	dismiss	dms
disgraced	dgrcd	disorder	dordr
disgraceful	dgrc^f	disparage	dprg / dprj
disgracefully	dgrc^{fy}	disparity	dprty
disguise	dgis	dispatch	dp$_c$
disguised	dgsd	dispatched	dp$_c$d
disguises	dgss	dispatches	dp$_c$s
disgust	dgst	dispel	dpl
disgusted	dgstd	dispelled	dpld
dish	d$_s$	dispensary	dpns^y
dishevelled	d$_s$vld	dispensation	dpns^n
dishonest	dhnst	dispense	dp^c
dishonestly	dhnst^y	dispersal	dprsl
disillusion	dil^n	disperse	dprs
disillusioned	dil^nd	displace	dplc
disillusionment	dil^{nm}	displaced	dplcd
disinfect	dinfct	display	dply / dpla
disinfectant	dinfctnt	displayed	dplyd
disinfected	dinfctd	displease	dpls
disintegrate	dingrt	disposable	dps^b
disintegrated	dingrtd	disposal	dpsl
disintegration	dingr^n	dispose	dps
disinterest	dintrst	disposition	dps^n
disjointed	djntd	dispossess	dpss
		dispossessed	dpssd

35

disproportion	$d$ppr^n	dissolve	$d$lv
disproportional	$d$ppr^{nl}	dissolved	$d$lvd
disproportionate	$d$ppr^{nt}	dissuade	$d$uad
disproportionately	$d$ppr^{nty}	dissuaded	$d$uadd
disprove	$d$prv	distance	dt^c
disputable	$d$pt^b	distanced	dt^{c}d
disputably	$d$pt^{by}	distances	dt^{c}s
dispute	$d$pt	distant	$d$nt
disputed	$d$ptd	distantly	$d$nt^y
disqualification	$d$qlfc^n	distaste	$d$tst
disqualified	$d$qlfd	distasteful	$d$tst^f
disqualify	$d$qlfy	distinct	$d$tnct
disregard	$d$rgrd	distinction	$d$tnc^n
disregarded	$d$rgrdd	distinctive	$d$tnctv
disrepair	$d$rpr	distinctiveness	$d$tnctvns
disreputable	$d$rpt^b	distinctly	$d$tnct^y
disrepute	$d$rput	distinctness	$d$tnctns
disrespect	$d$rspct	distinguish	$d$tngi$_s$
disrespectful	$d$rspct^f	distinguishable	$d$tng$_s$^{b}
disrupt	$d$rpt	distinguished	$d$tng$_s$d
disrupted	$d$rptd	distort	$d$trt
disruption	$d$rp^n	distortion	$d$tr^n
disruptive	$d$rptv	distract	$d$trct
dissatisfaction	$d$stsfc^n	distracted	$d$trctd
dissatisfactory	$d$stsfct^y	distractedly	$d$trctd^y
dissatisfied	$d$stsfd	distraction	$d$trc^n
dissatisfy	$d$stsfy	distracts	$d$trcts
disseminate	$d$smnat	distraught	$d$trt
disseminated	$d$smntd	distress	$d$trs
dissension	dn^n	distressed	$d$trsd
dissent	$d$nt	distressful	$d$trs^f
dissented	$d$ntd	distribute	$d$trbt
dissertation	$d$rt^n	distributed	$d$trbtd
disservice	$d$rvc	distributes	$d$trbts
dissimilar	$d$mlr	distribution	$d$trb^n
dissolution	$d$lu^n		

district	ᵈtrct	documentary	dc^my
distrust	ᵈtrst	dodge	dj
distrusted	ᵈtrstd	does	ds
distrustful	ᵈtrst^f	doesn't	dsnt
disturb	ᵈtrb	dog	dg
disturbance	ᵈtrb^c	doing	d^g
disturbances	ᵈtrb^c s	doll	dl
disturbed	ᵈtrbd	dollar	dlr
disturbing	ᵈtrb^g	dolphin	dlfn
disturbingly	ᵈtrb^gy	domain	dmn
disturbs	ᵈtrbs	domestic	dmstc
disused	ᵈusd	dominant	dmnnt
dither	d_t r	dominate	dmnt
diverge	dvrg	dominating	dmnt^g
divergence	dvrg^c	domination	dmn^n
divergent	dvrgnt	domineer	dmner
diverse	dvrs	don't	dnt
diversify	dvrsfy	donate	dnat
diversion	dvr^n	donation	dn^n
diversity	dvrsty	done	dn
divide	÷ / dvd	donor	dnr
divided	÷d / dvdd	door	dr
dividing	÷^g / dvd^g	doorway	drwy
divine	dvn	dose	ds / dos
divisible	÷^b / dvs^b	dot	dt / .
division	÷^n / dv^n	double	dbl / x2
divorce	dvrc	doubt	dbt
divorced	dvrcd	doubtful	dt^f
divulge	dvlg	dough	doh
DNA	dna	down	dn
do	do / d	downgrade	dngrd
doable	d^b	downgraded	dngrdd
dock	dk	download	dnld
doctor	dctr / dr	downloaded	dnldd
doctrine	dctrn	downplay	dnply
document	dc^m / doc	downsize	dnsz

downtown	dntn	duck	dk
dozen	dzn	due	du
draft	drft	dumb	dmb
drag	drg	dump	dmp
dragon	drgn	duplicate	dplct
drain	drn	duplication	dplc^n
drama	drma	durable	dr^b
dramatic	drmtc	duration	dra^n
dramatically	drmtc^y	duress	drs
draw	drw	during	dr^g
drawback	drwbck	dust	dst
drawer	drwr	Dutch	d_c
drawing	drw^g	dutiful	dti^f
drawn	drwn	duty	dty
dreadful	drd^f	dwelling	dwl^g
dream	drm	dye	dy / di
drench	drn_c	dying	dy^g
dress	drs	dynamic	dnmc
dried	drd	dynamics	dnmcs
drift	drft	dyscalculia	^dclcla
drill	drl	dysfunction	^dfnc^n
drink	drnk	dysfunctional	^dfnc^nl
drinkable	drnk^b	dyslexia	^dlxa
drinking	drnk^g	dyspraxia	^dprxa
drive	drv		
driven	drvn		
driver	drvr		
driveway	drvwy		
driving	drv^g		
drop	drp		
drown	drwn		
drug	drg		
drum	drm		
drummer	drmr		
drunk	drnk		
dry	d^y		

E

each	e_c
eager	egr
eagle	egl
ear	er
early	er^y
earmark	ermrk
earn	ern / urn
earning	ern^g
earnings	ern^{g}s
earshot	er$_s$t
earth	er$_t$
earthquake	er$_t$qk
ease	es
easement	es^m
easily	es^y
east	est
Easter	estr
eastern	estrn
easy	esy / ec
eat	et
eating	et^g
echo	e$_c$o
ecological	e^{o}cl
ecology	ec^o
economic	ecnmc
economically	ecnmc^y
economics	ecnmcs
economise	ecnms
economist	ecnmst
economy	ecnmy /econ
ecosystem	ecsstm

eczema	exma
edge	ej
edible	ed^b
edit	edt
edition	ed^n
editor	edtr
educate	edct
education	edc^n / edu
educational	edc^{nl}
educator	edctr
effect	efct
effective	efctv
effectively	efctv^y
effectiveness	efctvns
efficiency	ef^{cy}
efficient	efcnt
effluence	eflu^c
effort	efrt
egg	eg
ego	ego
eight	8
eighteen	18
eighth	8th / 8$_t$
eighty	80
either	e$_t$r
eject	ejct
elaborate	elbrt
elapse	elaps
elapsed	elapsd
elation	ela^n
elbow	elbo
elder	eldr
elderly	eldr^y
elect	elct
elected	elctd
election	elc^n

electric	elctrc	embrace	embrc
electrical	elctrcl / elec	emerge	emrg
electrician	eltr^n / elec^n	emergence	emrg^c
electricity	elctrcty	emergency	emrg^{cy}
electronic	elctrnc	emerging	emrg^g
electronics	elctrncs	emigration	emgra^n
elegance	elg^c	eminence	emn^c
elegant	elgnt	eminent	emnnt
element	el^m	emission	em^n
elemental	el^{ml}	emotion	emo^n
elementary	el^{my}	emotional	emo^{nl}
elephant	elfnt	emotionally	emo^{ny}
elevate	elvt	empathise	emp$_t$s
elevation	elv^n	empathy	emp$_t$y
elevator	elvtr	emperor	empr
eleven	11	emphasis	emphss/emfss
eleventh	11th /11$_t$	emphasise	emphsis
eligible	elg^b	empire	empr
eliminate	elmnat	employ	emply
elimination	elmn^n	employable	emply^b
elite	elt	employee	emplye
elongate	elngt	employment	emply^m
elongation	elnga^n	empower	empwr
eloquence	elq^c	empty	empt / mpt
eloquent	elqnt	emulate	emult
else	els	enable	en^b
elsewhere	els$_w$r	enact	enct
email	eml	enactment	enct^m
embankment	embnk^m	encampment	encmp^m
embargo	embrgo	enclose	encls / enc
embarrass	embrs	enclosed	enclsd / encd
embarrassed	embrsd	enclosure	enclsr
embassy	embsy/embsc	encounter	encntr
embezzle	embzl	encourage	encrg / encrj
embodiment	embdi^m	encouraging	encrg^g
embody	embdy	encroach	encr$_c$

encrypt	encrpt	enter	e
encrypted	encrptd	entered	^{e}d
encryption	encrp^n	enterprise	^{e}prs
end	nd	entertain	^{e}tn
endeavour	endvr	entertainment	^{e}tn^m
endless	endls	enthusiasm	en$_t$sism
endorse	endrs	enthusiastic	en$_t$sitc
endorsed	endrsd	entire	entr
endorsement	endrs^m	entirely	entr^y
endoscopy	enscpy	entitle	enttl
endow	endw	entitlement	enttl^m
endowment	endw^m	entity	enty
endurance	endr^c	entrance	entr^c
endure	endr	entrap	entrp
enemy	enmy	entrepreneur	entrprnr
energy	enrgy	entry	ent^y
enforce	enfrc	envelope	envlp
enforcement	enfrc^m	environment	envrn^m
engage	engg / engj	environmental	envrn^{ml}
engagement	engg^m	envision	env^n
engine	engn	epidemic	epdmc
engineer	engnr	epidermis	epdrms
engineering	engnr^g	epidural	epdrl
English	engl$_s$ / eng	episode	epsd
engulf	englf	equal / s	=
enhance	enh^c	equality	eqlty
enjoy	enjy	equally	eq^y
enjoyable	enjy^b	equate	eqt
enjoyment	enjy^m	equation	eq^n
enlarge	enlrg	equip	eqp
enlargement	enlrg^m	equipment	eqp^m
enormous	enrms	equity	eqty
enough	enf	equivalent	eqvlnt
enrol	enrl	era	era
enrolment	enrl^m	eradicate	erdct
ensure	en$_s$r	eradication	erdc^n

erase	eras	evaluate	evlut
erect	erct	evaluation	evlu^n
erection	erc^n	evaporate	evprt
erode	erod	evaporation	evpor^n
erosion	er^n	even	evn
error	err	evening	evn^g
escalate	esclt	event	evnt
escalating	esclt^g	eventful	evnt^f
escape	escp	eventually	evnt^y
Eskimo	eskmo	ever	evr
especially	esp^{sy}	evergreen	evgrn
essay	esy	everlasting	evrlst^g
essence	es^c	every	ev^y
essential	esn^s	everybody	ev^{y}bdy
essentially	esn^{sy}	everyday	ev^{y}dy
establish	estbl$_s$	everyone	ev^{y}on / ev^{y}1
established	estbl$_s$d	everything	ev^y_tg
establishment	estbl$_s^m$	everywhere	ev^y_wr
estate	estt	evict	evct
estimate	estmt / est	evicted	evctd
estimated	estmtd / estd	eviction	evc^n
estimation	estm^n	evidence	evd^c
etc	etc	evident	evdnt
etch	e$_c$	evidential	evdn^s
ethic	e$_t$c	evil	evl
ethical	e$_t$cl	evolution	evl^n
ethics	e$_t$cs	evolve	evlv
ethnic	e$_t$nc	exact	xct
ethnicity	e$_t$ncty	exactly	xct^y
ethos	e$_t$s	exam	xm
etiquette	etqt	examination	xmn^n
Europe	erop	examine	xmn
European	eropn	examined	xmnd
evacuate	evcut	examiner	xmnr
evacuation	evcu^n	example	xmpl / ex
evade	evd		

excavate	xcvt	exert	xrt
excavation	xcv^n	exerting	xrt^g
exceed	xcd	exertion	xr^n
excel	xl	exhale	xhl
excellence	xl^c	exhaust	xhst
excellent	xlnt	exhaustion	xhst^n
except	xcpt	exhibit	xhbt
exception	xcp^n	exhibition	xhb^n
exceptional	xcp^{nl}	exist	xst
excess	xcs	existence	xst^c
excessive	xsv	existing	xst^g
exchange	x$_c$ng	exit	xt
exchanged	x$_c$ngd	ex-officio	x-ofco
excitable	xcit^b	exonerate	xonr
excite	xcit	exonerated	xonrtd
excited	xcitd	exorbitant	xrbtnt
excitement	xcit^m	exotic	xotc
exciting	xcit^g	expand	xpnd
exclaimed	xclmd	expandable	xpnd^b
exclamation	xclm^n / !	expansion	xpn^n
exclude	xcld	expect	xpct
exclusion	xcl^n	expectation	xpct^n
exclusive	xclsv	expected	xpctd
exclusively	xclsv^y	expedient	xpdint
excrement	xcr^m	expedition	xpd^n
excursion	xcr^n	expendable	xpnd^b
excusable	xcs^b	expense	xp^c
excuse	xcs / xcus	expenses	xp^{c}s
excused	xcsd	expensive	xpnsv
execute	xct	experience	xpr^c
execution	xc^n	experienced	xpr^{c}d
executive	xctv / exec	experiment	xpri^m
exempt	xmpt	experimental	xpri^{ml}
exercise	xrcis / exer	expert	xprt
exercised	xrcisd	expertise	xprtis
exercising	xrcis^g	expiration	xpr^n

43

expire	xpr
explain	xpln
explained	xplnd
explanation	xpln^n
explicable	xplc^b
explicit	xplct
exploit	xplot
exploration	xplr^n
explore	xplr
explosion	xpl^n
export	xprt
expose	xps
exposure	xpsr
express	xprs
expression	xpr^n
expulsion	xpl^n
extend	xtnd
extended	xtndd
extension	xtn^n
extensive	xtnsv
extent	xtnt
extenuating	xtnut^g
external	xtrnl
extortionate	xtr^{n}t
extra	xtra
extract	xtrct
extraction	xtrc^n
extradite	xtrdit
extradition	xtrd^n
extraordinary	xtrordn^y
extreme	xtrm
extremely	xtrm^y
exuberance	xubr^c
eye	i
eyebrow	ibrw

F

fable	f^b
fabric	fbrc
fabrication	fbrc^n
face	fc / fs
facelift	fclft
facial	f^s
facilitate	fcltt
facilities	fclts
facility	fclty
fact	fct
factor	fctr
factory	fct^y
faculty	fclty
fade	fd
fail	fl / fal
failure	flr
faint	fnt
fair	fr
fairly	fr^y
faith	f$_t$
faithful	f$_t^f$
fall	fl
fallible	fl^b
false	fls
falsify	flsfy
fame	fm
familial	fmlil
familiar	fmlir
family	fm^y / fam
famous	fmos
fan	fn

fantastic	fntstc	feedback	fdbk
fantasy	fntsy	feel	fl / fel
far	fr	feeling	fl^g
fare	fr / far	fees	fs
farm	frm	feet	ft / fet
farmer	frmr	fell	fl
fascinate	fsnt	fellow	flw / flo
fascinating	fsnt^g	fellowship	flw^p
fascination	fsa^n	felt	flt
fashion	f$_s$n	female	fml / F / ♀
fashionable	f$_s$n^b	feminist	fmnst
fast	fst	fence	f^c
faster	fstr	fencing	f^{cg}
fat	ft	ferment	fr^m
fatal	ftl	festival	fstvl
fate	ft / fat	fetch	f$_c$
fateful	ft^f	fever	fvr
father	f$_t$r	few	fw
fatigue	ftig	fewer	fwr
fattening	ftn^g	fibre	fbr
fault	flt	fickle	fkl
faulty	flty	fiction	fc^n
favour	fvr	field	fld
favourable	fvr^b	fierce	frc
favourite	fvrt	fifteen	15
fax	fx	fifth	5th / 5$_t$
fear	fr	fifty	50
feasible	fs^b	fight	ft
feather	f$_t$r	fighter	ftr
feature	ftr	fighting	ft^g
February	fe	figure	fgr
federal	fdrl	figures	fgrs
federate	fdrt	file	fil
federation	fdr^n	fill	fl
fee	fe	film	flm
feed	fd		

45

filter	fltr	flatlining	fltln^g
fin	fn	flatten	fltn
final	fnl	flatter	fltr
finalise	fnlis	flatulence	fltul^c
finally	fn^y	flavour	flvr
finance	fn^c	flee	fle
financial	fnn^s	fleet	flt
find	fnd	flesh	fl_s
finding	fnd^g	flex	flx
fine	fn / fin	flexibility	flx^bty
finger	fngr	flexible	flx^b
finish	fn_s	flight	flt
fire	fr	flinch	fln_c
firm	frm	fling	fl^g
firmly	frm^y	flip	flp
first	frst / 1st	float	flt /flot
fiscal	fscl	flood	fld
fish	f_s	floor	flr
fisherman	f_s rmn	flotation	flot^n
fishing	f_s^g	flour	flr
fist	fst	flourish	flr_s
fistful	fst^f	flouting	flot^g
fit	ft	flow	flo
fitful	ft^f	flower	flwr
fitness	ftns	fluctuate	flctut
five	5	fluctuation	flctu^n
fix	fx	fluid	flid
fixation	fxa^n	fly	f^y
fixed	fxd	flying	f^yg
flag	flg	focus	fcs
flagship	flg^p	fog	fg
flamboyant	flmbynt	fold	fld
flame	flm	folk	flk
flamingo	flmngo	follow	flw / flo
flash	fl_s	following	flw^g
flat	flt	font	fnt

46

food	fod / fd	foretell	^{f}tl / 4tl
fool	fol / fl	foretold	^{f}tld / 4tld
foot	fot / ft	forever	^{f}evr / 4evr
football	ftbl	forewarn	^{f}wrn / 4wrn
for	^{f} / 4	forfeit	^{f}ft / 4ft
for example	eg	forfeited	^{f}ftd / 4ftd
for information	4 info / ^{f}infrm^n / ^{f}info	forfeiture	^{f}ftr / 4ftr
		forge	^{f}g / 4g
forbid	^{f}bd / 4bd	forged	^{f}gd / 4gd
forbidden	^{f}bdn / 4dbn	forget	^{f}gt / 4gt
force	^{f}c / 4c	forgetful	^{f}gt^f / 4gt^f
forced	^{f}cd / 4cd	forgettable	^{f}gt^b / 4gt^b
forceful	^{f}c^f / 4c^f	forgivable	^{f}gv^b / 4gv^b
forcefully	^{f}c^{fy} / 4c^{fy}	forgive	^{f}gv / 4gv
forcible	^{f}c^b / 4c^b	forgiveness	^{f}gvns / 4gvns
forcibly	^{f}c^{by} / 4c^{by}	forgo	^{f}go / 4go
foreboding	^{f}bd^g / 4bd^g	forgot	^{f}gt / 4gt
forecast	^{f}cst / 4cst	forgotten	^{f}gtn / 4gtn
forecaster	^{f}cstr / 4cstr	fork	^{f}k / 4k
foreclose	^{f}cls / 4cls	form	^{f}m / 4m
foreclosure	^{f}clsr / 4clsr	formal	^{f}ml / 4ml
forefront	^{f}frnt / 4frnt	formalise	^{f}mls / 4mls
forehead	^{f}fhd / 4hd	formally	^{f}m^y / 4m^y
foreign	^{f}n / 4n	format	^{f}mt / 4mt
foreigner	^{f}nr / 4nr	formation	^{f}m^n / 4m^n
foreigners	^{f}nrs / 4nrs	formed	^{f}md / 4md
foreman	^{f}mn / 4mn	former	^{f}mr / 4mr
forename	^{f}nm / 4nm	formerly	^{f}mr^y / 4mr^y
forensic	^{f}nsc / 4nsc	formula	^{f}mla / 4mla
forerunner	^{f}rnr / 4rnr	formulate	^{f}mlt / 4mlt
foresaw	^{f}sw / 4sw	formulation	^{f}mul^n / 4mul^n
foresee	^{f}se / 4nrse	fort	^{f}t / 4t
foreseeable	^{f}se^b / 4se^b	forth	^f_t / 4_t
foresight	^{f}st / 4st	forthcoming	^f_tcm^g / 4_tcm^g
forest	^{f}est / 4est		
foretaste	^{f}tst / 4tst		

fortify	ᶠtfy / 4tfy	freeway	frewy
fortnight	ᶠtnt / 4tnt	freeze	frz
fortunate	ᶠtunt / 4tunt	French	frn_c / fr
fortunately	ᶠtuntʸ / 4tuntʸ	frequency	frq^(cy)
fortune	ᶠtun / 4tun	frequent	frqnt
forty	40	frequently	frqntʸ
forum	ᶠum / 4um	fresh	fr_s
forward	ᶠwd / 4wd	freshman	fr_s mn
forwarded	ᶠwdd / 4wdd	friction	frcⁿ
foster	fstr	Friday	fr
found	fnd	friend	frnd
foundation	fndⁿ	friendly	frndʸ
founder	fndr	friendship	frndᵖ
four	4	fright	frt
fourteen	14	frightening	frtnᵍ
fourth	fr_t / 4th / 4_t	frightful	frtᶠ
fox	fx	frog	frg
fraction	frcⁿ	from	frm
fractional	frcⁿˡ	front	frnt
fracture	frctr	frontier	frntr
fragile	frgl	froth	fr_t
fragment	frgᵐ	frown	frwn
fragmented	frgᵐd	frozen	frzn
fragrance	frgrᶜ	fruit	frt
fragrant	frgrt	fruitful	frtᶠ
frame	frm / fram	fruition	fruiⁿ
framework	frmwrk	frustrate	frstrt
franchise	frn_c s	frustration	frstrⁿ
frankly	frnkʸ	fucking	fkᵍ
fraud	frd	fuel	ful
fraudulent	frdlnt	fulfil	flfl
fraught	fraut	fulfilment	flflᵐ
free	fre	full	fl
freedom	frdm	full-time	fltm
freelance	frlᶜ	fully	fʸ
freely	freʸ	fun	fn

function	fnc^n
functional	fnc^{nl}
fund	fnd
fundamental	fnd^{ml}
fundamentally	fnd^{my}
funding	fnd^g
fundraising	fndrs^g
funds	fnds
funeral	fnrl
fur	fr
furnish	frn$_s$
furniture	frntr
further	fr$_t$r
furthermore	fr$_t$rmr
fusion	f^n
futile	ftl
future	ftr / ftur

G

gain	gn
galaxy	glxy
gallery	gl^y
gamble	gmbl
game	gm
gang	gng
gap	gp
garage	grg / grj
garbage	grbg / grbj
garden	grdn
garlic	grlc
garment	gr^m
gas	gs
gasoline	gsln
gastric	gstrc
gate	gt
gather	g$_t$r
gathering	g$_t$r^g
gave	gv
gay	gy / ga
gaze	gz
gear	gr
gender	gndr
gene	gn
general	gnrl
generally	gnr^y
generate	gnrt
generation	gnr^n
generic	gnrc
generous	gnros
genetic	gntc
genius	gnus

49

genre	gnr	God	gd
gentle	gntl	going	g^g
gentleman	gntlmn	gold	gld
gently	gnt^y	golden	gldn
genuine	gnin	golf	glf
gerbil	grbl	gone	gn
German	grmn / gr	good	gd
gesture	gstr	gorilla	grla
get	gt	got	gt
ghost	gst	govern	gvrn
giant	gnt /gint	governance	gvrn^c
gibbon	gbn	government	gvrn^m / gov
gift	gft	governor	gvrnr
gifted	gftd	grab	grb
gimmick	gmk	grace	grc
giraffe	grf	graceful	grc^f
girl	grl	grade	grd
girlfriend	grlfrnd	gradual	grdul
girth	gr_t	gradually	grdu^y
give	gv	graduate	grdut / grad
given	gvn	graduation	grdu^n
glad	gld	graft	grft
glamour	glmr	grain	grn
glance	gl^c	grand	grnd
glare	glr	grandchild	grnd_cld
glass	gls	grandfather	grndf_tr
glimpse	glmps	grandmother	grndm_tr
glint	glnt	grandparent	grndprnt
glitch	gl_c	grant	grnt
global	glblglobe glb	grape	grp
glory	gl^y	graph	grf
glove	glv	graphical	grfcl
glucose	glcs	grasp	grsp
go	go / g	grass	grs
goal	gol / gl	grateful	grt^f
goat	got /gt	gratis	grts

grave	grv	guideline	gdln
gravel	grvl	guilt	glt
gravitate	grvtt	guilty	glty
gravitation	grvt^n	guitar	gtr /gitr
gravity	grvty	gullible	gl^b
gravy	grvy	gun	gn
great	grt	gut	gt
greater than	>	guy	gy
greatest	grtst / >	gym	gm
greatly	grt^y	gynaecology	gnc^o / gyn
Greek	grk / gr		
green	grn		
greet	gret		
grew	grw		
grey	gry		
grief	grf		
grievance	grv^c		
grieve	grv		
grin	grn		
grip	grp		
grocery	grc^y		
groom	grm		
gross	grs		
ground	grnd		
group	grp		
grow	grw / gro		
growing	grw^g / gro^g		
growth	grw$_t$		
gruelling	gruel^g		
guarantee	grnte		
guard	grd		
guardian	grdian		
guess	gs		
guest	gst		
guidance	gd^c		
guide	gd		

H

ha	ha
habit	hbt
habitable	hbt[b]
habitat	hbtt
habitation	hbt[n]
had	hd
hair	hr
hairdresser	hrdrsr
half	hlf / 1/2 / .5
halfway	hlfwy /1/2wy
hall	hl
hallmark	hlmrk
hallway	hlwy
hammer	hmr
hamster	hmstr
hand	hnd
handful	hnd[f]
handle	hndl
handover	hndovr/hnd[o]
handsome	hndsm
handwriting	hndrt[g]
hang	hng
happen	hpn
happened	hpnd
happily	hp[y]
happiness	hpns / hpins
happy	hpy
harass	hras
harassment	hras[m]
harbour	hrbr
hard	hrd
harden	hrdn
hardly	hrd[y]
hardship	hrd[p]
hardware	hrdwr
hardy	hrdy
harm	hrm
harmful	hrm[f]
harmony	hrmny
harsh	hr$_s$
harvest	hrvst
has	hs
hat	ht
hatch	h$_c$
hate	ht / hat
hateful	ht[f]
haul	hl /hal
hauler	hlir
have	hv
hay	hy /ha
hazard	hzrd
hazardous	hzrds/hzrdos
hazel	hzl
he	h
head	hd
headache	hda$_c$
headhunted	hdhntd
headhunter	hdhntr
headhunting	hdhnt[g]
headline	hdln
headquarters	hdqtrs
headship	hd[p]
heal	hl
health	hl$_t$
health-care	hl$_t$cr
healthy	hl$_t$y
hear	hr

52

heard	hrd	hide	hid
hearing	hr^g	hierarchy	hirr$_c$y / hirrky
heart	hrt	high	hi
heat	ht	highlight	hilt
heaven	hvn	highly	hi^y
heavily	hv^y	high-tech	hi-t$_c$ / hi-tk
heavy	hvy	highway	hiwy
hedge	hj / hg	hike	hk
heel	hl /hel	hill	hl
height	ht	him	hm
held	hld	himself	hmslf
helicopter	hlcptr /heli	hinder	hndr
hell	hl	hindrance	hndr^c
hello	hlo / hi	Hindu	hndu
helmet	hlmt	hint	hnt
help	hlp	hip	hp
helpdesk	hlpdsk	hire	hir
helpful	hlp^f	his	hs
hence	h^c	Hispanic	hspnc / hisp
her	hr	historian	hstrn
herb	hrb	historic	hstrc
here	hr / her	historical	hstrcl
heredity	hrdty	historically	hstrc^y
heritage	hrtg / hrtj	history	hst^y
hero	hro	hit	ht
heroine	hron	hitch	h$_c$
hers	hrs	hoard	hord
herself	hrslf	hockey	hky
hesitance	hst^c	hold	hld
hesitancy	hst^{cy}	hole	hl / hol
hesitant	hstnt	holiday	hldy
hesitate	hstt	hollow	hlo
hesitation	hst^n	holly	h^y / ho^y
hey	hy	holy	h^y
hi	hi	home	hm
hidden	hdn	homecoming	hmcm^g

53

homeland	hmlnd	hug	hg
homeless	hmls	huge	hj / hg
homework	hmwrk	huh	h
honest	hnst	human	hmn
honestly	hnst^y	human resources	hr / HR
honey	hny	humanity	hmnty
honour	hnr	humble	hm^b
honourable	hnr^b	humiliate	hmlit
hook	hk	humiliation	hmli^n
hope	hp	humour	hmr
hoped	hpd	hundred	100
hopeful	hp^f	hunger	hngr
hopefully	hp^{fy}	hungry	hng^y
horizon	hrzn	hunt	hnt
hormone	hrmn	hunter	hntr
horn	hrn	hunting	hnt^g
horrible	hr^b	hurricane	hrcn
horribly	hr^{by}	hurry	h^y
horrify	hrfy	hurt	hrt
horror	hrr	hurtful	hrt^f
horse	hrs	husband	hsbnd / hubi
hospitable	hspt^b	hydration	hdr^n
hospital	hsptl / hsp	hyperactive	hpractv/^{h}actv
host	hst	hypersensitive	hprsnstv / ^{h}snstv
hostage	hstg /hstj		
hostel	hstl	hypertension	hprtn^n / ^{h}tn^n
hostile	hostl	hyposensitive	hposnstv / $_h$snstv
hot	ht		
hotel	htl		
hour	hr	hypotension	hpotn^n/$_h$tn^n
hours	hrs	hypothesis	hpo$_t$s / $_{ht}$s
house	hs	hypothetical	hpo$_t$tcl / $_{ht}$tcl
household	hshld		
housing	hs^g		
how	hw		
however	hwevr		

I

I	i
ice	ic
ice cream	ic crm
icon	icn
idea	ida
ideal	idel
idealise	idels
identical	idntcl
identification	idntfc[n] / id
identified	idntfd
identifies	idntfs
identify	idntfy
identity	idntty
ideological	id°cl
ideology	id°
ie	ie
if	if
igloo	iglo
ignition	ign[n]
ignorance	ignr[c]
ignore	ignr
ill	il
illegal	ilgl
illicit	ilct
illness	ilns
illusion	il[n]
illustrate	ilstrt
illustrated	ilstrtd
image	imj / img
imaginable	imgn[b]/ imjn[b]
imagination	imgn[n] / imjn[n]
imagine	imgn / imjn
imbalance	imbl[c]
imitate	imtt
imitation	imt[n]
immediate	imdit
immediately	imdit[y]
immerse	imrs
immersion	imr[n]
immigrant	imgrnt
immigration	imgr[n]
imminent	imnnt
immovable	imv[b]
immune	imn
immunisation	imuns[n]
immunise	imuns
immunity	imnty
impact	impct
impair	impr
impairment	impr[m]
impartial	impr[s]
impassable	imps[b]
impatience	impa[c]
impatient	imp[n]t
impeccable	impc[b]
impede	imped
impediment	impd[m]
imperfect	imprfct
imperfection	imprfct[n]
impermeable	imprma[b]
implant	implnt
implausible	impls[b]
implement	impl[m]
implementation	impl[mn]
implicating	implct[g]
implication	implc[n]
implore	implr
implored	implrd

imply	imp^y	inch	in_c
import	imprt	incidence	incd^c
importance	imprt^c	incident	incdnt
important	imprtnt / imp	incision	inc^n
importantly	imprtnt^y/imp^y	inclement	incl^m
importation	imprt^n	inclination	incln^n
impose	imps	incline	incln
imposition	imps^n	include	incld
impossible	imps^b	including	incld^g
impotence	impt^c	inclusion	incl^n
impotent	imptnt	incoherent	inchrnt
impress	im^ps	income	incm
impressed	im^psd	incoming	incm^g
impression	im^pn	incompatible	in^cpt^b
impressive	im^psv	incompetence	in^cpt^c
imprison	imprsn	incorporate	incrprt
imprisoned	imprsnd	increase	incrs
improbable	im^pb^b	increased	incrsd
improbably	im^pb^by	increasing	incrs^g
improvable	im^pv^b	increasingly	incrs^gy
improve	im^pv	incredible	incrd^b
improved	im^pvd	incredibly	incrd^by
improvement	im^pvm	incubate	incubt
improvise	im^pvs	incubation	incub^n
imprudence	imprd^c	incurable	incr^b
impulse	impls	indecision	indcs^n
in	n	indeed	indd
in attendance	n-atnd^c	indefensible	indfns^b
inaccessible	inacs^b	indelible	indl^b
inactive	inctv	independence	indpnd^c
inadmissible	inadm^b	independent	indpndnt / indep
inadvisable	inadvs^b		
inaudible	inaud^b	index	indx
incapable	incp^b	indexation	indx^n
incarnation	incrn^n	Indian	indn / ind
incentive	insntv	indicate	indct

56

indicated	indctd	inflammable	inflm[b]
indication	indc[n]	inflatable	inflt[b]
indicator	indctr	inflation	infl[n]
indigenous	indgnos	inflexible	inflx[b]
indigestion	indgs[n]	influence	influ[c]
indignation	indgn[n]	influential	influn[s]
indirect	indrct	inform	infrm
individual	indvl /indiv	informal	infrml
indolence	indl[c]	information	inform[n] / info
indolent	indlnt	informed	infrmd
induce	indc	infrastructure	infrstrct
inducement	indc[m]	infrequent	infrqnt
induction	indc[n]	infringe	infrng / infrnj
indulge	indlg / indlj	infringement	infrng[m]
indulgence	indlg[c]	infuriate	infrit
industrial	indstrl	infuriation	infri[n]
industry	indst[y]	infuse	infus
inefficient	inefcnt	infusion	infu[n]
ineligible	inelg[b]	ingredient	ingrdnt
inertia	inrta	inhabit	inhbt
inescapable	inescp[b]	inhabitable	inhbt[b]
inevitable	inevt[b]	inhabiting	inhbt[g]
inevitably	inevt[by]	inhale	inhl
inexcusable	inxcs[b]	inhaling	inhl[g]
inexorable	inxr[b]	inherent	inhrnt
infallible	infl[b]	inherit	inhrt
infant	infnt	inheritance	inhrt[c]
infatuation	inftu[n]	inherited	inhrtd
infect	infct	inhibit	inhbt
infection	infc[n]	inhibition	inhb[n]
infer	infr	in-house	n-hs
inference	infr[c]	initial	in[s]
infest	infst	initialling	in[sg]
infestation	infst[n]	initially	in[sy]
infinite	infnt	initiate	intit
infinity	infnty / ∞	initiating	intit[g]

57

initiation	inti[n]	insistence	inst[c]
initiative	intitv	inspect	inspct
inject	injct	inspection	inspc[n]
injectable	injct[b]	inspector	ispctr / insp
injection	injct[n]	inspiration	inspr[n]
injunction	injnc[n]	inspire	inspr
injure	injr	install	instl
injuring	injr[g]	installation	instl[n]
injury	inj[y]	instalment	instl[m]
inmate	inmt	instance	inst[c]
inner	inr	instant	instnt
innocence	inc[c]	instantly	instnt[y]
innocent	incnt	instead	instd
innovation	inv[n]	instigate	instgt
innovative	invtv	instigation	instg[n]
innumerable	innmr[b]	instil	instl
inoculate	inoclt	instinct	instnct
inoculating	inoclt[g]	institution	instt[n]
inoperable	inopr[b]	institutional	instt[nl]
inpatient	n-p[n]_t	instruct	instrct
input	inpt	instruction	instrc[n]
inquiry	inq[y]	instructional	instrc[nl]
inquisition	inqs[n]	instructor	instrctr
inscribe	inscrb	instrument	instr[m]
inscription	inscrp[n]	insulate	inslt /inslat
insect	insct	insulating	inslt[g] / inslat[g]
insensible	insns[b]	insulation	insl[n]
inseparable	inspr[b]	insulin	insln
insert	insrt	insult	inslt
insertion	insr[n]	insulting	inslt[g]
inside	insd	insurable	insr[b]
insight	inst	insurance	insr[c]
insightful	inst[f]	insure	insr
insinuate	insnut	insurgence	insrg[c]
insinuation	insnu[n]	insurgency	insrg[cy]
insist	inst	insurgent	insgnt

intact	intct	interdental	[i]dntl
intangible	intng[b]	interdepartmental	[i]dpt[ml]
integrate	intgrt	interdependence	[i]dpnd[c]
integrated	intgrtd	interdependent	[i]dpndnt
integration	intgr[n]	interdivisional	[i]dv[nl]
integrity	intgry	interest	[i]st
intellectual	intlctl	interested	[i]std
intelligence	intlg[c] / intel	interesting	[i]st[g]
intelligent	intlgnt	interestingly	[i]st[gy]
intelligible	intlg[b]	interests	[i]sts
intend	intnd	interethnic	[i]etnc
intended	intndd	interface	[i]fc
intense	int[c]	interfaith	[i]ft
intensity	int[c]ty	interfamily	[i]fm[y]
intent	intnt	interfere	[i]fr
intention	intn[n]	interfered	[i]frd
intentionally	intn[nly]	interference	[i]fr[c]
interact	[i]act	intergeneration	[i]gnr[n]
interacted	[i]actd	intergenerational	[i]gnr[nl]
interaction	[i]ac[n]	interim	[i]m
interactive	[i]actv	interior	[i]ior
interbred	[i]brd	interject	[i]jct
interbreed	[i]bred	interjected	[i]jctd
intercede	[i]ced	interjection	[i]jct[n]
intercept	[i]cpt	interlace	[i]lc
intercepted	[i]cptd	interlaced	[i]lcd
interchange	[i][c]ng	interleave	[i]lv
interchangeable	[i][c]ng[b]	interlink	[i]lnk
intercom	[ic]	interlock	[i]lk
interconnect	[ic]ct	interlocked	[i]lkd
interconnection	[ic]c[n]	interlocutor	[i]lcutr
intercontinental	[ic]tntl	interlude	[i]ld
intercourse	[i]crs	intermarry	[i]m[y]
intercultural	[i]cltrl	intermediary	[i]mdi[y]
interdenominational	[i]dnmn[nl]	intermediate	[i]mdit
		interminable	[i]mn[b]

59

interminably	imnby	intervention	ivnn
intermingle	imngl	interview	ivw / ivu
intermission	imn	interviewed	ivwd
intermittent	imtnt	interviewee	ivwe
intermittently	imtnty	interviewer	ivwr
intermix	imx	interwove	iwv
intern	in	interwoven	iwvn
internal	inl	intestine	intstn
internalise	inlis	intimate	intmt
international	innl	into	into / in2
interned	ind	intolerable	intlrb
internet	int	intolerance	intlrc
internship	inp	intractable	iactb
interpersonal	iprsnl	intranet	iant
interplay	iply	intravenous	iavnos
interpret	iprt	intrigue	intrg
interpretation	iprtn	introduce	idc
interpreted	iprtd	introduces	idcs
interpreter	iprtr	introduction	idcn
interracial	irs	introductory	idcty
interregional	irgnl	introspection	ispcn
interregnum	irgnm	introvert	ivrt
interrelate	irlt	intrude	intrd
interrelationship	irlanp	intrusion	intrn
interrogate	irgt	intuition	intuin
interrogation	irgn	invade	invd
interrogator	irgtr	invalid	invld
interrupt	irpt	invaluable	invlub
interrupted	irptd	invariable	invrb
interruption	irpn	invasion	invn
intersect	isct	invent	invnt
intersection	iscn	invention	invnn
intersperse	isprs	inventory	invnty
intertwine	itwn	invest	invst
interval	ivl	investigate	invstgt
intervene	ivn	investigation	invstgtn

investigator	invstgtr	issue	isu
investment	invst^m	it	t
investor	invstr	it's / its	ts / its
invisible	invs^b	Italian	itln
invitation	invt^n	item	itm
invite	invt	iterate	itrat
invoice	invc	itinerary	itnr^y / intin
invoiced	invcd	itself	itslf
involve	invlv		
involved	invlvd		
involvement	invlv^m		
Iraqi	irq		
Ireland	irlnd / ir		
Irish	ir$_s$		
iron	irn		
ironically	irnc^y		
irony	irny		
irrelevance	irlv^c		
irrelevant	irlvnt		
irreparable	irpr^b		
irresistible	irsst^b		
irresponsible	irspns^b		
irreverence	irvr^c		
irreversible	irvrs^b		
irrigation	irg^n		
irritable	irt^b		
irritation	irt^n		
is	s		
Islam	islm		
Islamic	islmc		
island	ilnd		
isn't	snt / isnt		
isolate	islt		
isolated	isltd		
isolation	isl^n		
Israeli	isrli / is		

61

J

jacket	jkt
jaguar	jgr
jail	jl
January	ja
Japanese	jpns /jap
jar	jr
jargon	jrgn
jaw	jw
jazz	jz
jeans	jns
jeer	jer
jellyfish	j$^{yf}_s$
jet	jt
jettison	jtsn
Jew	jw
jewellery	jwl^y
Jewish	jw$_s$
job	jb
jobless	jbls
jog	jg
join	jn
joint	jnt
joke	jk
journal	jrnl
journalism	jrnlsm
journalist	jrnlst
journey	jrny
joy	jy
joyful	jy^f
joyriding	jyrd^g
jubilation	jbl^n
judge	jg / jj
judgement	jg^m / jj^m
judicial	jd^s
juice	jc
July	jl
jump	jmp
junction	jnc^n
June	jn
jungle	jngl
junior	jnr
jurisdiction	jrsdc^n
juror	jrr
jury	j^y
just	jst
justice	jstc
justifiable	jstfi^b
justify	jstfy

K

kangaroo	kngro /roo
keen	kn
keep	kp
kept	kpt
key	ky / ke
keyboard	kybrd
keynote	kynt
kick	kk
kid	kd
kidnap	kdnp
kidnapped	kdnpd
kidney	kdny
kill	kl
killer	klr
killing	kl^g
kind	knd
king	k^g
kingdom	k^{g}dm
kiss	ks
kit	kt
kitchen	k$_c$n
knead	ned
knee	ne
kneel	nel
knew	nw
knife	nf
knock	nk
know	no
knowledge	nolj / nolg
known	nwn
knows	nos
knuckle	nkl
koala	kla
Koran	krn
Korean	kren

L

lab	lb
label	lbl
laboratory	lbrt^y / lab
labour	lbr
labrador	lbrdr / lab
lacerate	lcrt / lsrt
laceration	lcrt^n
lack	lk
lactation	lct^n
lad	ld
ladder	ldr
laddish	ld$_s$
lady	ldy
ladybird	ldybrd
lake	lk
lament	l^m
laminate	lmnt
lamination	lmn^n
lamp	lmp
land	lnd
landfill	lndfl
landing	lnd^g
landlord	lndlrd
landmark	lndmrk
landowner	lndonr

63

landowning	lndon^g	leader	ldr
landscape	lndscp	leadership	ldr^p
lane	ln	leading	ld^g
language	lngj/lngg/lang	leaf	lf
languish	lngi_s	leaflet	lflt
lap	lp	league	lg
large	lrg / L	leak	lk
largely	lrg^y	lean	ln
laser	lsr	leap	lp
lass	ls	learn	lrn
last	lst	learning	lrn^g
lasted	lstd	lease	les
latch	l_c	least	lst / lest
late	lt	leather	l_t r
lately	lt^y	leave	lv
later	ltr / latr	leaver	lvr
lateral	ltrl	lecture	lctr
Latin	ltn	lecturer	lctrr
latter	ltr	led	ld
laugh	lgh / lf	left	lft
laughable	lgh^b / lf^b	leftwing	lftw^g
laughter	lghtr / lftr	leg	lg
launch	ln_c	legacy	lgcy
lavish	lv_s	legal	lgl
lavished	lv_s d	legalise	lglis
law	lw	legally	lg^y
lawbreaker	lwbrkr	legend	lgnd
lawbreaking	lwbrk^g	legible	lg^b
lawful	lw^f	legislate	lgslt
lawmaker	lwmkr	legislation	lgsl^n
lawn	lwn	legislative	lgsltv
lawsuit	lwst	legislator	lgsltr
lawyer	lwyr	legislature	lgsltur
lay	ly	legitimate	legtmt
layer	lyr	lemon	lmn
lead	ld	lend	lnd

64

length	lng$_t$	light	lt
lenience	lni^c	lighting	lt^g
lenient	lnint	lightly	lt^y
lens	lns	lightning	ltn^g
lesion	l^n	likable	lk^b
less	ls / <	like	lk
less than	<	likelihood	lklhd
lessen	lsn	likely	lk^y
lesser	lsr	liken	lkn
lesson	lsn / lson	likewise	lkws
let	lt	lilac	llc
letter	ltr	limb	lmb
level	lvl	limit	lmt
leverage	lvrj / lvrg	limitation	lmt^n
levied	lvd	limited	lmtd / ltd
levitate	lvtt	line	ln / lin
levy	lvy	link	lnk
liability	li^{bty}	lion	ln / lin
liable	li^b	lip	lp
liaise	lias	liquid	lqd
libel	lbl	list	lst
liberal	lbrl	listen	lstn
liberate	lbrt	listener	lstnr
liberation	lbr^n	listening	lstn^g
liberty	lbrty	literally	ltry / ltrl^y
library	lbr^y	literary	ltr^y
licence	lc^c	literature	ltrtr / lit
license	lc^c	litigate	ltgt
lid	ld	litigation	ltg^n
lie	li	litter	ltr
life	lf	little	ltl
lifestyle	lfstl	live	lv
lifetime	lftm	liver	lvr
lift	lft	living	lv^g
ligament	lg^m	lizard	lzd
ligature	lgtr	load	ld

loaded	ldd	loud	ld
loan	ln	lounge	lng / lnj
lobby	lby	lovable	lv^b
local	lcl	love	lv
localise	lclis	lovely	lv^y
locality	lclty	lover	lvr
locate	lcat	low	lw / lo
location	lc^n	lower	lwr
lock	lk	loyal	lyl
locked	lkd	loyalty	lylty
lodge	lj / lg	lubricate	lbrct
lodged	ljd / lgd	lubrication	lbrc^n
loft	lft	luck	lk
log	lg	lucky	lky
logic	lgc	lucrative	lcrtv
logical	lgcl	lunch	ln$_c$
loin	ln / lon	lung	lng
loiter	ltr	lush	l$_s$
lone	ln / lon	lust	lst
lonely	ln^y	lustful	lst^f
long	lng	lying	ly^g
long-term	lng-trm		
longtime	lngtm		
look	lk		
loop	lp		
loophole	lphl		
loose	ls / los		
loosen	lsn		
looter	ltr		
looting	lt^g		
lose	ls / los		
loss	ls		
lost	lst		
lot	lt		
lotion	l^n		
lots	lts		

M

machine	m$_c$n
mad	md
maddening	mdn^g
made	md
magazine	mgzn / mag
magic	mgc
magnate	mgnt
magnet	mgnt
magnetic	mgntc
magnify	mgnfy
magnitude	mgntd
magpie	mgpi
mail	ml
main	mn
mainly	mn^y
mainstream	mnstrm
maintain	mntn
maintenance	mntn^c
major	mjr
majority	mjrty
make	mk
makeover	mk^o
maker	mkr
makeup	mkup
male	ml/ M / ♂
malfunction	mlfnc^n
malignancy	mlgn^{cy}
malignant	mlgnnt
malinger	mlngr
mall	ml
maltreat	mltrt
mammal	mml
mammoth	mm$_t$
man	mn
manage	mng / mnj
manageable	mng^b
management	mng^m
manager	mngr
managing	mng^g
mandate	mndt
mandatory	mndt^y
manhandle	mnhndl
manhandled	mnhndld
manifest	mnfst
manipulate	mnplt
manner	mnr
manoeuvre	mnvr
manoeuvred	mnvrd
mansion	mn^n
manufacture	mnfctr/manu
manufacturer	mnfctrr
manufacturing	mnfctr^g
many	mny
map	mp
maple	mpl
mapped	mpd
marble	mrbl
march	mr$_c$
March	ma
margin	mrgn
marginal	mrgnl
marine	mrn
mark	mrk
marked	mrkd
marker	mrkr
market	mrkt / mkt
marketable	mrkt^b

67

marketing	mrkt^g	meaning	mn^g
marketplace	mktplc	meaningful	mn^{gf}
maroon	mron	meant	mnt
marriage	mrg / mrj	meantime	mntm
married	mrd	meanwhile	mn$_w$l
marrow	mrw	measurable	msr^b
marry	m^y	measure	msr
marshal	mr$_s$l	measurement	msr^m
marvel	mrvl	meat	mt
mash	m$_s$	mechanic	m$_c$nc / mech
mask	msk	mechanical	m$_c$ncl
mass	ms	mechanism	m$_c$nsm
massage	msj / msg	medal	mdl
massive	msv	media	mda
master	mstr	mediate	mdit
match	m$_c$	mediation	mdi^n
matchbox	m$_c$bx	medical	mdcl
mate	mt	medicate	mdct
material	mtrl / mtril	medication	mdc^n
maternity	mtrnty / mat	medicine	mdcn
mathematics	m$_t$mtcs/maths	mediocre	mdocr
maths	m$_t$s	meditate	mdtt
matter	mtr	meditation	mdt^n
mature	mtur	medium	mdm /med
matured	mturd	meet	mt
maturely	mtur^y	meeting	mt^g
maximise	mxmis	melody	mldy
maximum	mxm / max	melt	mlt
May	my	member	mbr
may	ma / my	members	mbrs
maybe	myb	membership	mbr^p
mayor	myr	membrane	mbrn
me	m	memo	mo
meal	ml	memorable	mr^b / mem^b
mean	mn	memorandum	mo / memo
meander	mendr		

memorised	mrsd / memd	mild	mld
memory	m^y / mem	mile	ml
men	mn	milestone	mlstn
mend	mnd	militant	mltnt
menial	mnil	military	mlt^y
mental	mntl	milk	mlk
mentally	mnt^y	mill	ml
mention	mn^n	million	mln / 10^6
mentioned	mnnd	millionaire	mlnar
mentor	mntr	mind	mnd
mentored	mntrd	mindset	mndst
menu	mnu	mine	mn / min
merchandise	mr$_c$nds	mineral	mnrl
merchant	mr$_c$nt	mingle	mngl
mere	mr	minimal	mnml
merely	mr^y	minimise	mnmis
merge	mrg	minimum	mnm / min
merit	mrt	minister	mnstr
mess	ms	ministry	mnst^y
message	msg / msj	minor	mnr
metal	mtl	minority	mnrty
metaphor	mtfr	minute	mnt / mn
meter	mtr	minutes	mnts / mns
method	m$_t$d	minute-taker	mnt-tkr m/t
methodology	m$_t$d^o	miracle	mrcl
metropolitan	mtrpltn/metro	mirror	mrr
Mexican	mxcn /mx	misadvise	msadvs
microbiology	mcrbi^o	misalign	msalgn
microscope	mcrscp	misbehave	msbhv
microwave	mcrwv	miscellaneous	mclnos/misc
middle	mdl / mid	misconduct	ms^{c}dct
midnight	mdnt	miscounted	mscntd
midst	mdst	misdirect	msdrct
midwife	mdwf	miserable	msr^b
might	mt	misgiving	msgv^g
migration	mgr^n	misguided	msgdd

mishandle	mshndl	mole	ml / mol
mislead	msled	molecular	mlclr
misled	msld	molecule	mlcl
mismatch	msm$_c$	molest	mlst
misplace	msplc	mom	m
misquote	msqt	moment	m^m
miss	ms	momentum	m^{m}m
missed	msd	Monday	mo
missile	msl	money	mny
missing	ms^g	moneymaking	mnymk^g
mission	m^n	mongrel	mngrl
missionary	m^{ny}	monitor	mntr
mistake	mstk	monkey	mnky
mistaken	mstkn	monster	mnstr
mistreat	mstrt	month	mn$_t$
mistrust	mstrst	monthly	mn$_t^y$
mitigate	mtgt	monument	mnu^m
mitigation	mtg^n	mood	md
mix	mx	moon	mn / mon
mixed	mxd	moose	ms /mos
mixture	mxtr	moral	mrl
mm-hmm	m-hm	more	mr
moan	mon	moreover	mr^o
mobile	mbl / mob	moribund	mribnd
mode	md /mod	morning	mrn^g
model	mdl	mortality	mrtlty
modelled	mdld	mortgage	mrgg/ mrgj/ mrg
modem	mdm		
moderate	mdrt	most	mst
moderation	mdr^n	mostly	mst^y
moderator	mdrtr	moth	m$_t$
modern	mdrn	mothballed	m$_t$bld
modernise	mdrnis	mother	m$_t$r
modest	mdst	motion	m^n
modification	mdfc^n	motivate	mtvt
modify	mdfy		

motivation	mtv^n	multiscreen	^{m}scrn
motive	mtv	multisensory	^{m}sns^y
motor	mtr	multi-storey	^{m}st^y
motorised	mtrsd	multitalented	^{m}tlntd
mount	mnt	multitasking	^{m}tsk^g
mountain	mntn / mt	multivitamins	^{m}vtmns/^{m}vits
mouse	mos	mumble	mbl
mouth	m$_t$	municipal	mncpl
move	mv	murder	mrdr
movement	mv^m	murdered	mrdrd
movie	mve	murmur	mrmr
Mr	mr	muscle	msl
Mrs	mrs	museum	msm
Ms	ms	mushroom	m$_s$rm
much	m$_c$	music	msc
mucus	mucs	musical	mscl
mud	md	musician	ms^n
muddy	mdy	Muslim	mslm
mule	ml /mul	must	mst
multicolour	^{m}clr	mutate	mutt
multicoloured	^{m}clrd	mute	mut
multicultural	^{m}cltrl	mutter	mtr
multidisciplinary	md plny	mutual	mtl
multifunction	^{m}fnc^n	my	my
multifunctional	^{m}fnc^{nl}	myself	myslf
multilateral	^{m}ltrl	mysterious	mstros
multi-lingual	^{m}lngl	mystery	mst^y
multimedia	^{m}mda	myth	m$_t$
multimillion	^{m}mln		
multipack	^{m}pk		
multiplayer	^{m}plyr		
multiple	^{m}pl		
multiplication	^{m}plc^n		
multiply	^{m}p^y		
multipurpose	^{m}prps		
multiracial	^{m}r^s		

N

nag	ng
nail	nl
naked	nkd
name	nm
named	nmd
narcotic	nrctc
narrate	nrt
narrative	nrtv
narrator	nrtr
narrow	nrw / nro
nasal	nsl
nasty	nsty
natal	ntl
nation	n^n
national	n^{nl}
nationwide	n^{n}wd
native	ntv
natural	ntrl
naturally	ntr^y
nature	ntr
nausea	nsa
nauseating	nsat^g
navigable	nvg^b
navigate	nvgt
navigation	nvg^n
navigational	nvg^{nl}
Neanderthal	nndr$_t$l
near	nr
nearby	nrby
nearly	nr^y
neat	nt
nebuliser	nbulsr / neb
necessarily	ncsr^y
necessary	ncs^y
necessity	ncsty
neck	nk
need	nd
needle	ndl
negate	ngat
negative	ngtv / -
neglect	nglct
neglectful	nglct^f
negligence	nglg^c
negligible	nglg^b
negotiable	ngot^b
negotiate	ngott
negotiation	ngot^n
neighbour	nbr
neighbourhood	nbrhd
neighbouring	nbrg
neither	n$_t$r
neonatal	nontl / neo
nerve	nrv
nervous	nrvos
nest	nst
net	nt
network	ntwrk
neural	nrl
neutral	ntrl
never	nvr
nevertheless	nvr$_t$ls
new	nw
newly	nw^y
news	nws
newspaper	nwspr
next	nxt
nice	nc

nicotine	nctin	nose	ns
niggle	ngl	not	nt
night	nt	note	nt / nb
nightmare	ntmr	notebook	ntbk
nine	9	noted	ntd
nineteen	19	note-taker	ntkr
ninth	9th / 9_t	nothing	$n_t{}^g$ / 0
nip	np	notice	ntc
nipple	npl	noticeable	ntc^b
nitpicking	ntpk^g	notified	ntfyd
no	no / x	notify	ntfy
nobody	nbdy	notion	n^n
nod	nd	notional	n^{nl}
noise	nos	noun	nn / non
nominate	nmnt	nourish	nr$_s$
nomination	nmn^n	nourishing	nr$_s{}^g$
nominee	nmne	nourishment	nr$_s{}^m$
nonchalance	nn$_c$l^c	novel	nvl
nonchalant	nn$_c$lnt	now	nw
none	nn	nowhere	n$_w$r
nonetheless	nn$_t$ls	nuance	nu^c
non-executive	nn-xctv / nxec	nuclear	nclr
non-payer	nnpyr	nuisance	nus^c
non-paying	nnpy^g	nullify	nlfy
nonprofit	nnprft	numb	nm
non-voting	nnvt^g	number	no / nmbr
noon	nn / 12	numeral	nmrl
nor	nr	numerous	nmros
norm	nrm	nuptial	np^s
normal	nrml	nurse	nrs
normalise	nrmls	nut	nt
normally	nrm^y	nutrient	ntrnt
north	nr$_t$ / n	nutrition	ntr^n
northeast	ne	nutritional	ntr^{nl}
northern	nr$_t$n	nutritious	ntrtos
northwest	nw		

73

O

o'clock	oclk
oak	ok
oath	o_t
obedience	obd^c
obedient	obdnt
obese	obs
obey	oby
object	objct
objection	objct^n
objective	objctv / obj
obligation	oblg^n
oblige	oblg / oblj
obscure	obscr
obscured	obscrd
observation	obsrv^n
observe	obsrv
observer	obsrvr
obsess	obss
obsession	obs^n
obsessive	obssv
obsolete	obslt
obstacle	obstcl
obstruct	obstrct
obstruction	obstrc^n
obtain	obtn
obtainable	obtn^b
obvious	obvos
obviously	obvos^y
occasion	oca^n
occasional	oca^nl
occasionally	oca^ny
occupation	ocp^n / occ
occupy	ocpy
occur	ocr
occurrence	ocr^c
ocean	o^n
October	oc
octopus	octps
odd	od
odds	ods
of	f
off	of
offence	of^c
offend	ofnd
offender	ofndr
offense	of^c
offensive	of^cv
offer	ofr
offered	ofrd
offering	ofr^g
office	ofc
officer	ofcr
official	of^s
officially	of^sy
offload	ofld
offloaded	ofldd
offset	ofst
offspring	ofspr^g
often	oftn / oft
oh	o
oil	ol
ok	ok / k
okay	ok / k
old	old
old-fashioned	old-f_snd
Olympic	olpc
Olympics	olpcs

omission	omi^n	optimal	optml
omit	omt	optimised	optmsd
on	on / o / n	optimistic	optmstc
once	o^c	option	op^n
oncologist	onclgst	optional	op^{nl}
oncology	onc^o	options	op^{n}s
one	1	or	or
one-half	1/2	oral	orl
one-quarter	1/4	orally	or^y
one-third	1/3	orange	orng
ongoing	ong^g	orangu-tan	orngtn
onion	onn	orbit	orbt
online	onln	ordain	ordn
onlooker	onlkr	order	ordr
only	on^y	ordinary	ordn^y /ordin
onto	on2	organ	orgn
open	opn	organic	orgnc
opening	opn^g	organisation	orgns^n
openly	opn^y	organisational	orgns^{nl}
opera	opra	organise	orgnis
operable	opr^b	organised	orgnsd
operate	oprt	organism	orgnsm
operating	oprt^g	orientating	orintt^g
operation	opr^n / op	orientation	orint^n
operator	oprtr	orienting	orint^g
opinion	opnn / opn	origin	orgn
opponent	opnt	original	orgnl
opportunity	oprtnty / opp	originally	orgn^y
oppose	ops	origination	orgn^n
opposed	opsd	ornament	orn^m
opposite	opst	orthopaedic	or$_t$pdc / or$_t$o
opposition	opos^n	ostrich	ostr$_c$
oppressed	oprsd	other	o$_t$r
oppression	oprs^n	others	o$_t$rs
opt	opt	otherwise	o$_t$rws
opted	optd	otter	otr

ought	ot	oven	ovn
our	r	over	o
ours	rs	overachieve	ºa_cv
ourselves	rslvs	overact	ºact
oust	ost	overall	ºal
out	ot	overarching	ºar_cg
outbid	otbd	overbalance	ºbl^c
outclass	otcls	overbearing	ºbr^g
outclassed	otclsd	overcautious	ºctos
outcome	otcm	overcome	ºcm
outdated	otdtd	overdo	ºdo
outdistance	otdst^c	overdose	ºds
outdo	otdo	overdraft	ºdrft
outdoing	otd^g	overdue	ºdu
outdoor	otdr	overflow	ºflw
outer	otr	overfunding	ºfnd^g
outfit	outft	overgrow	ºgrw
outgoing	otg^g	overhang	ºhng
outgrow	otgro	overhear	ºhr
outlast	otlst	overhype	ºhp
outlawed	otlwd	overlap	ºlp
outlet	otlt	overlay	ºly
outline	otln	overload	ºld
outlined	otlnd	overlook	ºlk
outlived	otlvd	overnight	ºnt
outplacement	otplc^m	overpay	ºpy
outpouring	otpr^g	overpayment	ºpy^m
output	otpt	overreact	ºact
outreach	otr_c	overreaction	ºac^n
outsell	otsl	override	ºid
outside	otsd	overrule	ºul
outsider	otsdr	oversee	ºse / ºc
outsource	otsrc	overshadow	º_sdw
outstanding	otstnd^g	oversight	ºst
outwit	owt	overstate	ºstt
outwith	otw_t	overstay	ºsty

overtake	ᵒtk		
overtrade	ᵒtrd		
overview	ᵒvw / ᵒvu		
overweight	ᵒwt		
overwhelm	ᵒ_wlm		
overwhelming	ᵒ_wlmg	pace	pc
overworked	ᵒwrkd	pacemaker	pcmkr
overwritten	ᵒrtn	pacify	pcfy
ovulation	ovulⁿ	pack	pk
owe	ow	package	pkg / pkj
owl	ol /owl	pact	pct
own	own	pad	pd
owner	ownr	paediatric	pdtrc / ped
ownership	ownrᵖ	page	pg / pj
oxygen	O₂ / ox / oxy	pain	pn
oyster	ostr	painful	pnᶠ
		painkiller	pnklr
		paint	pnt
		painter	pntr
		painting	pntᵍ
		pair	pr
		palace	plc
		pale	pl
		Palestinian	plstnn
		palm	plm
		palpitation	plptⁿ
		pamper	pmpr
		pan	pn
		panda	pnda
		panel	pnl
		panic	pnc
		pant	pnt
		paper	ppr
		parade	prd
		paragraph	prgrf / para
		parallel	prll

P

paralyse	prlys	patch	p$_c$
paramedic	prmdc	patent	ptnt
parameter	prmtr	path	p$_t$
parcel	prcl	pathology	p$_t$^{o}
parent	prnt	patience	ps^c
parental	prntl	patient	psnt
parish	pr$_s$	patrol	ptrl
parity	prty	patron	ptrn
park	prk	patronage	ptrnj / ptrng
parking	prk^g	patronise	ptrnis
parliament	prli^m	pattern	ptrn
part	prt	pause	ps
partial	pr^s	pavement	pv^m
partially	pr^{sy}	pawn	pwn
participant	prtcpnt	pay	py / pa
participate	prtcpt	payable	py^b / pa^b
participation	prtcp^n	payback	pybk / pabk
particle	prtcl	payment	py^m / pa^m
particular	prtclr / part	PC	pc
particularly	prtclr^y	peace	pec / pes
partition	prt^n	peaceful	pec^f
partly	prt^y	peach	p$_c$
partner	prtnr	peak	pk
partnership	prtnr^p	peanut	pnt
party	prty	peasant	psnt
pass	ps	peel	pl
passable	ps^b	peer	pr
passage	psg /psj	pen	pn
passenger	psgr /psjr	penalty	pnlty
passing	ps^g	pence	p^c
passion	p^n	pencil	pncl
past	pst	pending	pnd^g
pasta	psta	penetrate	pntrt
paste	past	penetration	pntr^n
pastor	pstr	penguin	pngn
pat	pt		

pension	pn^n	personal	^{p}snl
pensionable	pn^{nb}	personality	^{p}snlty
people	ppl	personally	^{p}sn^y
pepper	ppr	personnel	^{p}snel
per	p	perspective	^{p}spctv
perceive	^{p}cv	perspiration	^{p}spr^n
perceived	^{p}cvd	persuade	^{p}sad
percentage	^{p}cntg / %	persuasion	^{p}sa^n
perceptible	^{p}cpt^b	perverse	^{p}vrs
perception	^{p}cp^n	perversely	^{p}vrs^y
perfect	^{p}fct	perversion	^{p}vr^n
perfection	^{p}fct^n	pervert	^{p}vrt
perfectly	^{p}fct^y	pester	pstr
perforate	^{p}frt	pet	pt
perforation	^{p}fr^n	petition	pt^n
perform	^{p}frm	pharmacy	phrmcy / frmcy/ pharm
performance	^{p}frm^c		
performer	^{p}frmr	phase	phs / fs
perhaps	^{p}hps	phenomenon	phnmnn / fnmnn
period	^{p}id		
peripheral	^{p}frl	philosophical	phlosfcl / flosfcl
perish	p$_s$		
perjury	^{p}jy	philosophy	ph^o / f^o
perk	^{p}k	phone	phn / fn
permanent	^{p}mnnt	phony	phny / fny
permeate	^{p}mat	photo	phto / fto
permission	^{p}m^n	photograph	phtogrph / ftogrf /photo
permit	^{p}mt		
persecute	^{p}scut	photographer	phtogrphr / ftogrfr
persecution	^{p}scu^n		
persevere	^{p}sver	photography	phtogrphy / ftogrfy
Persian	pn		
persist	^{p}sst	phrase	phrs / frs
persistence	^{p}sst^c	physical	phscl / fscl
person	^{p}sn	physically	phsc^y / fsc^y
		physician	phs^n / fs^n

physics	phscs / fscs	pizza	pza
physiology	phsi° / fsi°	place	plc
physiotherapy	phsi o$_t$rpy / fsio$_t$rpy/physio	placement	plc^m
		plain	plan
piano	pno	plan	pln
pick	pk	plane	plan
picked	pkd	planet	plnt / plnet
picketing	pkt^g	planned	plnd
pickup	pkup	planner	plnr
picture	pctr / pic	planning	pln^g
pie	pi	plant	plnt
piece	pes	plastic	plstc
pierce	pierc	plate	plt
pig	pg	plateau	pltu
pigeonhole	pjnhl	platform	pltfrm
pigment	pg^m	plausible	pls^b
pile	pl /pil	play	ply
pilfer	plfr	player	plyr
pill	pl	playoff	plyof
pillow	plw / plo	plea	ple
pilot	plt	plead	pld
pin	pn	pleasant	plsnt
pinch	pn$_c$	please	pls
pine	pn / pin	pleased	plsd
pink	pnk	pleasurable	plsr^b
pinpoint	pnpnt	pleasure	plsr
pioneer	pionr	pledge	plj / plg
pip	pp	plentiful	plnt^f
pipe	pp /pip	plenty	plnty
pipeline	ppln	pliable	pli^b
pit	pt	plot	plt
pitch	p$_c$	plug	plg
pitcher	p$_c$r	plumber	plmr
pitiful	pt^f	plumbing	plm^g
pittance	pt^c	plummet	plmt
pivot	pvt	plunge	plng

plural	plrl	population	ppl^n
plus	+	porch	pr$_c$
PM	pm	pork	prk
poach	po$_c$	port	prt
pocket	pkt	portable	prt^b
poem	pm / pom	portfolio	prtflo
poet	pot	portion	pr^n
poetry	ptry	portrait	prtrt
point	pnt	portray	prtry
pointed	pntd	pose	ps
poison	posn	position	ps^n
poisoned	posnd	positive	pstv / +
poke	pk	possess	pss
pole	pl	possession	ps^n
police	plc	possibility	ps^{bty} / pos
policeman	plcmn	possible	ps^b
policewoman	plcwmn	possibly	ps^{by}
policy	plcy	post	pst
Polish	pl$_s$	postdated	pstdtd
polish	pl$_s$	poster	pstr
political	pltcl	postmarked	pstmrkd
politically	pltc^y	postnatal	pstntl
politician	plt^n	postpone	pstpn
politics	pltcs	pot	pt
poll	pl	potato	pto
pollinate	plnat	potential	ptn^s
pollute	plut	potentially	ptn^{sy}
pollution	pl^n	pound	pnd / £ / lb
pond	pnd	pour	pr
ponder	pndr	poverty	pvrty
pool	pl / pol	powder	pwdr
poor	pr / por	power	pwr
pop	pp	powered	pwrd
popular	pplr	powerful	pwr^f
popularity	pplrty	practicable	prctc^b
populate	pplt	practical	prctcl

practically	prctc^y	precocious	p^ccos
practice	prctc	preconceive	p^ccv
practise	prcts	preconceived	p^ccvd
practitioner	prct^nr	precondition	p^cd^n
praise	prs	predate	pdt
pray	pry	predator	pdtr
prayer	pryr	predatory	pdt^y
pre admission	p^adm^n	predecease	pdces
pre adult	p^adlt	predestined	pdstnd
pre approve	p^aprv	predicament	pdc^m
pre book	p^bk	predict	pdct
pre check	p^ck	predictable	pdct^b
pre order	p^ord	predictably	pdct^by
pre treat	p^trt	predicted	pdctd
preach	p_c	prediction	pdc^n
preacher	p_c r	predisposed	p^dpsd
preamble	p^ambl	predominance	pdmn^c
prearrange	p^arng	predominant	pdmnnt
prearranged	p^arngd	preeminent	p^emnnt
precancerous	p^cncros	preempt	p^empt
precarious	p^cros	preexist	p^xst
precariously	p^cros^y	preexistence	p^xst^c
precaution	p^c^n	prefabricate	p^fbrct
precautionary	p^c^ny	preface	p^fc
precede	p^ced	prefect	p^fct
preceded	p^cedd	prefer	p^fr
precedence	p^cd^c	preferable	p^fr^b
precedent	p^cdnt	preferably	p^fr^by
precinct	p^cnct	preference	p^fr^c
precious	p^cos	preferential	p^frn^s
precipitate	p^cptt	preferred	p^frd
precipitated	p^cpttd	prefix	p^fx
precise	p^cs	pregnancy	prgn^cy
precisely	p^cs^y	pregnant	p^gnnt / preg
precision	p^c^n	prehistoric	p^hstrc
preclude	p^cld	prejudge	p^jg / p^jj

82

prejudice	pjdc	presided	psdd
prejudicial	pjds	presidency	psdcy
preliminary	plmny	president	psdnt / pres
premature	pmtr	presidential	psdns
prematurely	pmtry	press	ps
premier	pmir	pressure	p_sr
premiership	pmirp	pressured	p_srd
premise	pms	prestige	pstg
premium	pmum	presumably	psmby
premonition	pmnn	presume	psm
preoccupied	pocpd	presumed	psmd
preparation	ppran	presumption	psmpn
prepare	ppr	presuppose	psps
prepared	pprd	presupposition	pspsn
prepay	ppy	pretence	ptc
prepayment	ppym	pretend	ptnd
preplanned	pplnd	pretended	ptndd
preponderance	ppndrc	pretentious	ptntos
preregister	prgstr	pretty	pty / prty
prescribe	pscrb	prevail	pvl
prescription	pscrpn	prevailed	pvld
prescriptive	pscrptv	prevalence	pvlc
preselect	pslct	prevalent	pvlnt
presence	psc	prevaricate	pvrct
present	psnt	prevent	pvnt
presentable	psntb	preventable	pvntb
presentably	psntby	preventative	pvnttv
presentation	psntn	prevention	pvnn
presented	psntd	preview	pvw / pvu
presenter	psntr	previous	pvos
presently	psnty	previously	pvosy
preservation	psrvn	prewarm	pwrm
preserve	psrv	prey	py / pry
preserved	psrvd	price	prc
preset	pst	priceless	prcls
preside	psd	prick	prk

83

pride	prd	probably	p^bby
priest	prst	probation	pbⁿ
priggish	prg_s	probe	prb
primacy	prmcy	probed	prbd
primal	prml	problem	pblm
primarily	prmr^y	problematic	pblmtc
primary	prm^y	procedural	pcdrl
prime	prm	procedure	pcdr
primitive	prmtv	proceed	pcd
principal	prncpl	proceeded	pcdd
principle	prncpl	proceeds	pcds
principled	prncpld	process	pcs
principles	prncpls	processes	pcss
print	prnt	processing	pcs^g
printable	prnt^b	procession	psⁿ
printer	prntr	processor	pssr
printout	prntot	proclaim	pclm
prior	pror	procrastinate	pcrstnt
priorities	prorts	procrastination	pcrstnⁿ
prioritise	prorts	procure	pcr
priority	prorty	procurement	pcr^m
prison	prsn	prodigy	pdgy
prisoner	prsnr	produce	pdc
privacy	prvcy	produced	pdcd
private	prvt	producer	pdcr
privately	prvt^y	produces	pdcs
privation	prvaⁿ	product	pdct
privatise	prvtis	production	pdcⁿ
privatised	prvtsd	productive	pdctv
privilege	prvlg / prvlj	productivity	pdctvty
privileged	prvlgd	profanity	pfnty
prize	prz	profess	pfs
pro	p	profession	pfsⁿ
proactive	pactv	professional	pfs^{nl}
probability	p_bbty	professionally	pfs^{nly}
probable	p_b^b	professor	pfsr

proffer	pfr	promising	pms^g
proficiency	pf^ncy	promote	pmt
proficient	pf^nt	promotion	pm^n
profile	pfl	promotional	pm^nl
profit	pft	prompt	pmpt
profitability	pft^bty	promptly	pmpt^y
profitable	pft^b	prone	pn
profligate	pflgt	pronounce	pn^c
profound	pfnd	pronounced	pn^cd
profuse	pfs	pronouncement	pn^cm
prognosis	pgnss	pronunciation	pnca^n
program	pgrm	proof	pf
programme	pgrmd	proofread	pfrd
programmed	pgrmd	propaganda	ppgnda
programmer	pgrmr	propagate	ppgt
programming	pgrm^g	propel	ppl
progress	pgrs	proper	ppr
progression	pgr^n	properly	ppr^y
progressive	pgrsv	property	pprty
progressively	pgrsv^y	prophesy	pfsy
prohibit	phbt	prophetic	pftc
prohibition	phb^n	proponent	ppnnt
prohibitive	phbtv	proportion	pp^n
project	pjct	proportional	pp^nl
projected	pjctd	proportionality	pp^nlty
projection	pjc^n	proportionally	pp^nly
projector	pjctr	proportionate	pp^nt
proliferate	plfrt	proportions	ppr^ns
proliferation	plfr^n	proposal	ppsl
prolific	plfc	propose	pps
prominence	pmn^c	proposed	ppsd
prominent	pmnnt	proposer	ppsr
prominently	pmnnt^y	proposition	pps^n
promiscuity	pmscuty	proprietor	pprtr
promiscuous	pmscus	prosaic	psc
promise	pms	prosecute	psct

prosecution	psc{n}	proverbial	pvbl
prosecutor	psctr	provide	pvid
prospect	pspct	provided	pvidd
prospective	pspctv	providence	pvd{c}
prospects	pspcts	provider	pvdr
prospectus	pspctus	province	pv{c}
prosper	pspr	provincial	pvn{s}
prosperous	pspros	provision	pv{n}
prostate	pstt	provisional	pv{nl}
prosthetic	ps{t}tc	proviso	pvso
prostitute	psttut	provocation	pvc{n}
prostrate	ptrt	provocative	pvctv
protect	ptct	provoke	pvk
protected	ptctd	provoked	pvkd
protection	ptc{n}	prowl	pwl
protective	ptctv	proximity	pxmty
protectively	ptctv{y}	proxy	pxy
protein	pten	prudence	prd{c}
protest	ptst	prudent	prdnt
protestant	ptstnt	psychiatrist	sciatrst
protester	ptstr	psychological	sclgcl
protocol	ptcl	psychologist	sclgst
prototype	pttyp	psychology	psyc{o} / sc{o}
protract	ptrct	puberty	pbrty
protracted	ptrctd	public	pblc
protrude	ptrud	publication	pblc{n}
protruded	ptrudd	publicity	pblcty
protrusion	ptru{n}	publicly	pblc{y}
protuberance	ptbr{c}	publish	pbl{s}
proud	pd	publisher	pbl{s}r
proudly	pd{y}	publishing	pbl{s}{g}
prove	prv	pull	pl
proved	prvd	pulmonary	plmn{y}
proven	pvn	pulse	pls
provenance	pvn{c}	pump	pmp
proverb	pvrb	punch	pn{c}

punctual	pnctl	quench	qn_c
punctuation	pncta^n	querying	qry^g
punish	pn_s	quest	qst
punishable	pn_s^b	question	?
punishment	pn_s^m	questionable	?^b
pupil	ppl	questioning	?^g
purchase	pr_c s	questionnaire	?ar
pure	pr /pur	queue	q
purple	prpl	quick	qk
purpose	prps	quicken	qkn
purse	prs	quickly	qk^y
pursue	prsu	quiet	qet
pursuit	prst	quietly	qet^y
push	p_s	quit	qt
put	pt	quite	qit
puzzle	pzl	quiver	qvr
		quorate	qrt
		quorum	qrm
		quota	qta
		quotation	qta^n
		quote	qot
		quotient	qtint
		Quran	qrn

Q

qualification	qlfc^n / qual
qualify	qlfy
quality	qlty
quantify	qntfy
quantity	qnty
quarantine	qrntn
quarrel	qrl
quart	qrt
quarter	1/4
quarterback	qrtrbk
quash	q_s
queen	qn
quell	ql

R

rabbit	rbt
raccoon	rcn
race	rc
racial	r^s
racism	rcsm
rack	rk
radar	rdr
radiance	rd^c
radiant	rdint
radiate	rdit
radiation	rdi^n
radical	rdcl
radio	rdo
radiography	rdogrphy / rdogrfy
radiotherapy	rdo$_t$rpy
raffle	rfl
rage	rg
raid	rd
rail	rl
railroad	rlrd
rain	rn
raise	rs
raised	rsd
rally	r^y
ramble	rmbl
ramification	rmfc^n
rampage	rmpg / rmpj
ran	rn
ranch	rn$_c$
random	rndm
randomised	rndmisd
range	rng
rank	rnk
ranked	rnkd
ransom	rnsm
rant	rnt
rape	rp
raped	rpd /rapd
rapid	rpd
rapidly	rpd^y
rapture	rptr
rare	rr
rarely	rr^y / r^y
rash	r$_s$
rasp	rsp
raspberry	rspbry
rat	rt
ratchet	r$_c$t
rate	rt
rather	r$_t$r
ratify	rtfy
rating	rt^g
ratio	rto
ration	rs^n
rational	r^{nl}
rationale	r^{n}al
rattle	rtl
ravage	rvg / rvj
raw	rw
razor	rzr
re	r /re
reabsorb	rabsrb
reach	r$_c$
react	ract
reaction	rac^n
reactive	ractv

read	rd	rebuke	rbuk
reader	rdr	recall	rcl
readership	rdr[p]	recalled	rcld
readily	rd[y]	recap	rcp
reading	rd[g]	recapture	rcptr
readjust	rajst	recede	rced
readmission	radm[n]	receipt	rcpt
readmit	radmt	receive	rcv
ready	rdy	received	rcvd
reaffirm	rafrm	receiver	rcvr
real	rl	receivership	rcvr[p]
realign	raln	recent	rcnt
realignment	raln[m]	recently	rcnt[y]
realise	rals	reception	rcp[n]
realistic	ralstc	recess	rcs
reality	ralty	recession	rcs[n]
really	r[y]	recharge	r$_c$rg
realm	rlm	recipe	rcp
reappear	rapr	recipient	rcpnt
reapply	rap[y]	reckon	rkn
rear	rr	reclaim	rclm
rearrange	rarng	reclamation	rclm[n]
rearrest	rarst	recline	rcln
reason	rsn	recognise	rcgns
reasonable	rsn[b]	recognition	rcgn[n]
reassert	rasrt	recollect	rclct
reassess	rass	recommend	rcmnd
reassign	rasin	recommendation	rcmnd[n]
reassurance	rasr[c]	reconcile	rcncl
reassure	rasr	reconstruct	r[c]strct
rebalance	rbl[c]	record	rcrd
rebate	rbt	recording	rcrd[g]
rebel	rbl	recoup	rcop
rebound	rbnd	recover	rcvr
rebuff	rbf	recovery	rcv[y]
rebuild	rbld	recreate	rcret

89

recreating	rcret[g]	reflection	rflc[n]
recreation	rcre[n]	reflex	rflx
recreational	rcre[nl]	reflux	rflx
recruit	rcrt	refocus	rfcs
recruitment	rcrt[m]	reform	rfrm
rectify	rctfy	refrain	rfrn
rector	rctr	refresh	rfr[s]
recuperate	rcprt	refreshment	rfr[s][m]
recur	rcr	refrigerator	rfrgrtr/frg /frj
recurrence	rcr[c]	refuel	rful
recycle	rcycl	refuge	rfg / rfj
red	rd	refugee	rfge / rfje
redact	rdct	refund	rfnd
redeem	rdem	refurbish	rfrb[s]
redefine	rdfn	refurbishment	rfrb[s][m]
redeploy	rdply	refuse	rfs
redeploying	rdply[g]	regain	rgn
redirect	rdrct	regard	rgrd
redouble	rdbl	regarding	rgrd[g]
redraft	rdrft	regardless	rgrdls
redress	rdrs	regime	rgm
reduce	rdc	regiment	rg[m]
reduction	rdc[n]	region	rgn / rjn
redundant	rdndnt / rdnt	regional	rgnl
re-emergence	remrg[c]	register	rgstr
reenact	renact	registrar	rgstrr
reenaction	renac[n]	regrade	rgrad
re-evaluate	revlut	regress	rgrs
refer	rfr	regression	rgr[n]
referee	rfre	regret	rgrt
reference	rfr[c]	regroup	rgrp
referred	rfrd	regular	rglr
refinance	rfn[c]	regularly	rglr[y]
refine	rfn	regulate	rglt
refit	rft	regulated	rgltd
reflect	rflct	regulation	rgl[n]

regulator	rgltr	relegate	rlgt
regulatory	rglt^y	relegation	rlg^n
rehabilitation	rhblt^n	relent	rlnt
rehearsal	rhrsl	relevance	rlv^c
rehearse	rhrs	relevant	rlvnt
rehome	rhm	reliability	rli^bty
rehomed	rhmd	reliable	rli^b
rehouse	rhs	reliance	rli^c
rehydrate	rhydrt	relief	rlf
rehydration	rhydr^n	relieve	rlv
reimburse	rimbrs	religion	rlgn
reindeer	rndr	religious	rlgos
reinfection	rinfct^n	relish	rl$_s$
reinforce	rinfrc	relocate	rlct
reinstate	rinstt	relocation	rlc^n
reinvent	rinvnt	reluctant	rlctnt
reinvest	rinvst	rely	r^y
reiterate	ritrat	remain	rmn
reject	rjct	remaining	rmn^g
rejection	rjct^n	remark	rmrk
rejoice	rjc	remarkable	rmrk^b
rekindle	rkndl	rematch	rmt$_c$
relabel	rlbl	remedial	rmdil
relapse	rlps	remedy	rmdy
relate	rlt	remember	rmbr / rem
related	rltd	remembrance	rmbr^c
relation	rl^n	remind	rmnd
relationship	rla^np	reminded	rmndd
relative	rltv	reminder	rmndr
relatively	rltv^y	remission	rm^n
relativity	rltvty	remittance	rmt^c
relaunch	rln$_c$	remorseful	rmrs^f
relax	rlx	remote	rmt
relaxation	rlx^n	removal	rmvl
relaxing	rlx^g	remove	rmv
release	rles	renal	rnl

91

render	rndr	representative	rᵖsntv / rep
renounce	rnnᶜ	repress	rᵖs
renovate	rnvt	repression	rᵖⁿ
renovation	rnvⁿ	reprieve	rprv
renown	rnwn	reprint	rprnt
rent	rnt	reproachful	rᵖ_c ᶠ
rental	rntl	reproduce	rᵖdc
renumbering	rnmbrᵍ	republic	rpblc
reoccupy	rocpy	Republican	rpblcn
reopen	ropn	repulsive	rplsv
reoperate	roprt	reputable	rptᵇ
reorder	rordr	reputation	rptⁿ
repackage	rpkg / rpkj	request	rqst
repair	rpr	require	rqr
reparation	rprⁿ	required	rqrd
repay	rpy	requirement	rqrᵐ
repayment	rpyᵐ	rescue	rscu
repeat	rpt	research	rsr_c
repeated	rptd	researcher	rsr_c r
repeatedly	rptdʸ	reselect	rslct
repel	rpl	resell	rsl
repetition	rptⁿ	reseller	rslr
replace	rplc	resemble	rsmbl
replaceable	rplcᵇ	resentful	rsntᶠ
replacement	rplcᵐ	reservation	rsrvⁿ
replay	rply	reserve	rsrv
replicate	rplct	reshuffle	r_s ᶠ
replies	rpls	residence	rsdnᶜ
reply	rpʸ	resident	rsdnt
report	rprt	residential	rsdnˢ
reported	rprtd	resign	rsn
reportedly	rprtdʸ	resignation	rsgnⁿ
reporter	rprtr	resilience	rslᶜ
reporting	rprtᵍ	resilient	rslnt
represent	rᵖsnt	resist	rsst
representation	rᵖsntⁿ		

resistance	rsst[c]	resuscitation	rsct[n]
resolution	rsl[n]	retail	rtl
resolve	rslv	retailer	rtlr
resolved	rslvd	retain	rtn
resonance	rsn[c]	retaliate	rtlit
resort	rsrt	retard	rtrd
resound	rsnd	retch	r[c]
resource	rsrc	retention	rnt[n]
resourceful	rsrc[f]	rethink	r[t]nk
respect	rspct	retire	rtr
respectable	rspct[b]	retired	rtrd
respectful	rspct[f]	retirement	rtr[m]
respectfully	rspct[fy]	retouch	rt[c]
respectively	rspctv[y]	retract	rtrct
respiration	rspr[n]	retractable	rtrct[b]
respiratory	rsprt[y]	retraction	rtrc[n]
respond	rspnd	retrain	rtrn
respondent	rspndnt	retreat	rtrt
response	rsp[c]	retribution	rtrb[n]
responsibility	rspn[bty]	retrieve	rtrv
responsible	rspn[b]	retrospect	rtrspct
responsibly	rspn[by]	retrospective	rtrspctv
rest	rst	retrospectively	rtrspctv[y]
restaurant	rstrnt	return	rtrn
restful	rst[f]	reunite	runt
restoration	rstr[n]	reusable	rus[b]
restore	rstr	reuse	rus
restrain	rstrn	revamp	rvmp
restrict	rstrct	reveal	rvl
restriction	rstrc[n]	revelation	rvl[n]
restroom	rstrm	revenge	rvng / rvnj
result	rslt	revenue	rvnu
resume	rsm	reverence	rvr[c]
resurface	rsrfc	reverse	rvrs
resurgence	rsrg[c]	reversible	rvrs[b]
resuscitate	rsctt	reversing	rvrs[g]

93

revert	rvrt	ring	r^g
review	rwv	ringfence	r^{g}f^c
reviewed	rvwd	riot	riot
revise	rvis	rip	rp
revision	rv^n	rise	rs
revisit	rvst	risen	rsn
revive	rvv	risk	rsk
revoke	rvk	risky	rsky
revolution	rvlu^n	ritual	rtl
revolutionary	rvlu^{ny}	rival	rvl
revolve	rvlv	river	rvr
revulsion	rvl^n	road	rd
rewaken	rawkn	roadholding	rdhld^g
reward	rwrd	roadmap	rdmp
reword	rwrd	roam	rm
rewritten	rrtn	rob	rb
rhetoric	rtrc	robbed	rbd
rhinoceros	rnocrs	robber	rbr
rhyme	rym	robin	rbn
rhyming	rym^g	robot	rbt
rhythm	r$_t$m	rock	rk
rib	rb	rocket	rkt
ribbon	rbn	rod	rd
rice	rc	role	rl / rol
rich	r$_c$	roll	rl
rid	rd	rolling	rl^g
ride	rd / rid	Roman	rmn
rider	rdr	romance	rm^c
ridge	rg / rj	romantic	rmntc
ridicule	rdcul	roof	rf
ridiculous	rdculos	room	rm
riding	rd^g	root	rt
rifle	r^f	rope	rp
right	rt	rose	rs
rightful	rt^f	rotate	rtt
rim	rm	rotation	rt^n

94

rough	rf
roughly	rf^y
round	rnd
route	rt /rot
routine	rtn
routinely	rtn^y
row	rw
royal	ryl
rub	rb
rubber	rbr
ruin	run
rule	rl
ruling	rl^g
rumble	rmbl
rumour	rmr
run	rn
runner	rnr
running	rn^g
rupture	rptur
rural	rrl
rush	r_s
Russian	rsⁿ
rust	rst

S

sabotage	sbtg / sbtj
sack	sk
sacred	scrd
sacrifice	scrfc
sad	sd
sadly	sd^y
safe	sf
safekeeping	sfkp^g
safely	sf^y
safety	sfty
said	sd
sail	sl
sake	sk
salad	sld
salary	sl^y
sale	sl / sal
sales	sls
salient	slint
saliva	slva
salmon	smn / slmn
salt	slt
salute	slut
salvage	slvg / slvj
same	sm
sample	smpl
sampling	smpl^g
sanction	sncⁿ
sand	snd
sandwich	sndw_c
sanitised	sntsd
sat	st
satellite	stlt

satisfaction	stsfc^n	school	scl
satisfactory	stsfct^y / sat	science	si^c
satisfy	stsfy	scientific	sintfc
saturate	strt	scientist	sintst
saturation	stra^n	scold	scld
Saturday	sa	scope	scp
sauce	sc	scorch	scr$_c$
savage	svg / svj	score	scr
save	sv	scorn	scrn
saver	svr	Scotland	sctlnd / sct
saving	sv^g	scramble	scrmbl
savour	svr	scrap	scrp
savoury	sv^y	scrape	scrap
savvy	svy	scratch	scr$_c$
saw	sw	scream	scrm
say	sy / sa	screen	scrn
saying	sy^g	screening	scrn^g
scald	scld	screw	scrw
scale	scl	scribble	scrbl
scan	scn	scribe	scrb
scandal	scndl	script	scrpt
scandalise	scndlis	scrub	scrb
scanner	scnr	scrutinise	scrtns
scar	scr	scuffle	scfl
scare	scr /scar	sculpt	sclpt
scared	scrd	sculpture	sclptr
scary	sc^y	sea	c
scatter	sctr	seahorse	chrs
scavenge	scvng / scvnj	seal	sl
scenario	scnro	search	sr$_c$
scene	scn	season	ssn
scent	snt	seat	st
schedule	scdl	seclusion	scl^n
scheme	scm	second	scnd / 2nd
scholar	sclr	secondary	scnd^y / 2nd^y
scholarship	sclr^p	seconded	scndd / 2ndd

96

seconder	scndr / 2ndr	semblance	smbl^c
secondment	scnd^m / 2nd^m	semi-detached	smi-dt$_c$d
seconds	2nd / secs	seminar	smnr
secret	scrt	Senate	snt / snat
secretary	scrt^y	senator	sntr
section	sc^n	send	snd
sectioned	sc^{n}d	senior	snr
sector	sctr	sensation	sns^n
secular	sclr	sensational	sns^{nl}
secure	scr	sense	s^c
securely	scr^y	sensitive	snstv
security	scrty	sensitivity	snstvty
sedate	sdt	sent	snt
sediment	sd^m	sentence	snt^c
seduction	sdc^n	sentencing	snt^{cg}
see	c	sentiment	snt^m
seed	sd / cd	separate	sprt
seeing	c^g	separation	spr^n
seek	sk	September	se
seem	sm	sequence	sq^c
seemingly	sm^{gy}	sequential	sqn^s
seethe	s$_t$	sergeant	srgnt
segment	sg^m	serialise	srials
segregate	sgrgt	series	srs
segregation	sgrg^n	serious	sros
seize	sz	seriously	sros^y
seizure	szr	servant	srvnt
seldom	sldm	serve	srv
select	slct	service	srvc
selected	slctd	serving	srv^g
selection	slc^n	session	s^n
self	slf	set	st
self-esteem	slf-estm	setback	stbk
selfish	slf$_s$	setting	st^g
sell	sl	settle	stl
seller	slr	settlement	stl^m

settling	stl^y	sheath	$_s$st
seven	7	shed	$_s$d
seventeen	17	sheep	$_s$p
seventh	7th / 7$_t$	sheer	$_s$r
seventy	70	sheet	$_s$t
sever	svr	shelf	$_s$lf
several	svrl	shell	$_s$l
severance	svr^c	shelter	$_s$ltr
severe	svr	shelve	$_s$lv
severely	svr^y	shelving	$_s$lv^g
sex	sx	shepherd	$_s$prd
sexual	sxul / sxl	sheriff	$_s$rf
sexuality	sxulty / sxlty	shield	$_s$ld
sexually	sx^y	shift	$_s$ft
sexy	sxy	shine	$_s$n / $_s$in
shade	$_s$d	shingles	$_s$ngls
shaded	$_s$dd	ship	$_s$p / $_s$p
shades	$_s$ds	shipment	^{pm} / $_s$p^m
shadow	$_s$dw	shipping	^{pg} / $_s$p^g
shake	$_s$k	shirk	$_s$rk
shall	$_s$l	shirt	$_s$rt
shallow	$_s$lw	shit	$_s$t
shambles	$_s$mbls	shiver	$_s$vr
shame	$_s$m	shock	$_s$k
shameful	$_s$m^f	shoe	$_s$o
shape	$_s$p	shoestring	$_s$ostr^g
share	$_s$r	shoot	$_s$t / $_s$ot
shared	$_s$rd	shooting	$_s$t^g / $_s$ot^g
shareholder	$_s$rhldr	shop	$_s$p
shark	$_s$rk	shoplift	$_s$plft
sharp	$_s$rp	shopper	$_s$pr
sharpen	$_s$rpn	shopping	$_s$p^g
sharply	$_s$rp^y	shore	$_s$r
shave	$_s$v	short	$_s$rt
she	sh / s	shortage	$_s$rtj / $_s$rtg
sheaf	$_s$f		

shortbread	ₛrtbrd	sift	sft
shortcoming	ₛrtcmᵍ	sigh	sgh / si
shorten	ₛrtn	sight	st
shortfall	ₛrtfl	sign	sn
shortly	ₛrtʸ	signage	sng / snj
shorts	ₛrts	signal	sgnl
short-term	ₛrt-trm	signature	sgntr / sig
shot	ₛt	significance	sgnfᶜ
should	ₛd	significant	sgnfcnt
shoulder	ₛldr	significantly	sgnfcntʸ
shout	ₛt	signify	sngfy
shove	ₛv	signpost	snpst
shovel	ₛvl	Sikh	sk / skh
show	ₛw / ₛo	silence	slᶜ
showcasing	ₛwcsᵍ	silent	slnt
shower	ₛwr	silk	slk
shred	ₛrd	silly	sʸ
shrewd	ₛrwd	silver	slvr
shrimp	ₛrp	similar	smlr
shrink	ₛnk	similarity	smlrty
shrivel	ₛrvl	similarly	smlrʸ
shrug	ₛtg	simmer	smr
shudder	ₛdr	simple	smpl
shuffle	ₛfl	simplify	smplfy
shut	ₛt	simply	smpʸ
shutter	ₛtr	simulate	smult
shuttle	ₛtl	simultaneously	smltnosʸ / sim
shy	ₛy	sin	sn
sibling	sblᵍ	since	sᶜ
sick	sk	sinful	snᶠ
sicken	skn	sing	sᵍ
side	sd	singer	sᵍr
sideline	sdln	single	sᵍl
sidewalk	sdwlk	sink	snk
siege	sg / sj	sir	sr
		sister	sstr / sis

99

sit	st	slick	slk
site	st / sit	slide	sld /slid
situation	stua^n	slight	slt
six	6	slightly	slt^y
sixteen	16	slimline	slmln
sixth	6th / 6$_t$	sling	sl^g
sixty	60	slip	slp
size	sz	slippage	slpg / slpj
skeleton	skltn	slither	sl$_t$r
ski	ski	slogan	slogn
skid	skd	slope	slop
skilful	skl^f	slot	slt
skill	skl	sloth	sl$_t$
skilled	skld	slow	slw / slo
skim	skm	slowly	slw^y /slo^y
skin	skn	slug	slg
skip	skp	sluggish	slg$_s$
skirt	skrt	sluice	slc
skive	skv	slumber	slmbr
skulking	sklk^g	slump	slmp
skull	skl	slur	slr
skunk	sknk	smack	smk
sky	sky	small	sml
slack	slk	smart	smrt
slacken	slkn	smash	sm$_s$
slam	slm	smattering	smtr^g
slander	slndr	smell	sml
slant	slnt	smile	sml / smil
slap	slp	smiling	smil^g
slash	sl$_s$	smirk	smrk
slave	slv	smoke	smk
slavery	slv^y	smoking	smk^g
sleep	slp	smooth	sm$_t$
sleeve	slv	smother	sm$_t$r
slender	slndr	smoulder	smldr
slice	slc	smuggle	smgl

snack	snk	solder	sldr
snail	snl	soldier	sldier / sljr
snake	snk /snak	sole	sl
snap	snp	solely	sl^y
snatch	sn$_c$	solicitor	slctr
sneak	snk	solid	sld
sneakers	snks	solution	sl^n
sneaky	snky	solve	slv
sneer	snr	solving	slv^g
sneeze	snz	some	sm
snivel	snvl	somebody	smbdy
snore	snr	someday	smdy
snow	sno	somehow	smhw
so	so	someone	smon / sm1
soak	sk	something	sm$_t$^{g}
soar	sr	sometime	smtm
sob	sb	sometimes	smtms
sober	sbr	somewhat	sm$_w$t
so-called	so-cld	somewhere	sm$_w$r
soccer	scr	son	sn
social	s^s / so^s	song	sng
socialised	s^{s}lsd	soon	sn / son
socialising	s^{s}ls^g	sophisticated	sfstctd
socially	s^{sy}	sorry	s^y
society	scty	sort	srt
sock	sk	soul	sl /sol
socket	skt	sound	snd
sodium	sdm / na	soup	sp / sop
sofa	sfa	source	src
soft	sft	south	s$_t$ / s
soften	sfn	southeast	se
softly	sft^y	southern	s$_t$rn
software	sftwr	southwest	sw
soil	sol	sovereignty	svrnty
solar	slr	Soviet	svt
sold	sld	sow	sw

space	spc	spirit	sprt
spaniel	spnl	spiritual	sprtl
Spanish	spn$_s$	spit	spt
spare	spr	spite	spit
spark	sprk	spiteful	spt^f
sparrow	sprw / spro	splash	spl$_s$
spatial	sp^s	splint	splnt
speak	spk	split	splt
speaker	spkr	spoke	spk
spec	spc	spokesman	spksmn
special	sp^s	spokesperson	spksprsn
specialise	sp^{s}s	spokeswoman	spkswmn
specialist	spst	sponsor	spnsr
specialty	sp^{sty}	sponsorship	spnsr^p
species	spcs	spoon	spn / spon
specific	spcfc	sport	sprt
specifically	spcfc^y	sporty	sprty
specify	spcfy	spot	spt
spectacular	spctclr	spouse	sps /spos
spectra	spctra	spray	spry
spectroscopy	spctrscpy	spread	sprd
spectrum	spctrm	spring	spr^g
speculate	spclt	sprinkle	sprnkl
speculation	spcl^n	sprint	sprnt
speech	sp$_c$	spy	spy
speed	spd	squad	sqd
spell	spl	squander	sqndr
spend	spnd	square	sqr / □
spending	spnd^g	squash	sq$_s$
sphere	sfr	squeeze	sqz
spill	spl	squint	sqnt
spin	spn	squirm	sqrm
spinal	spnl	squirrel	sqrl
spine	spn / spin	stabilise	st^{b}s
spinster	spnstr	stability	st^{bty}
spiral	sprl	stable	st^b

102

stack	stk	statute	sttt
stadium	stdm /stad	stay	sty
staff	stf	steadily	std^y
stage	stg / stj	steady	stdy
stagger	stgr	steak	stk / stek
staggering	stgr^g	steal	stl / stel
stagnate	stgnat	steam	stm
stair	str	steel	stl / stel
stairway	strwy	steep	stp / step
stake	stk	steer	str /ster
stalemate	stlmt	stem	stm
stance	st^c	step	stp
stand	stnd	stereotype	strotp
standard	stndrd	sterile	stril
standing	stnd^g	sterilise	strlis
staple	stpl	steroid	stroid
star	str	steward	stwrd
stare	str / star	stick	stk
start	strt	stiff	stf
starter	strtr	still	stl
starting	strt^g	stimulate	stmlt
startle	strtl	stimulus	stmls
starvation	strv^n	sting	st^g
starve	strv	stink	stnk
state	stt	stipulate	stpult
stated	sttd	stipulation	stpul^n
statement	stt^m	stir	str
static	sttc	stitch	st$_c$
station	st^n	stock	stk
stationary	st^{ny}	stocking	stk^g
stationery	st^{ny}	stockpile	stkpl
statistic	sttstc / stat	stocktake	stktk
statistical	sttstcl	stomach	stm$_c$
statistics	sttstcs / stats	stone	stn
statue	sttu	stood	std
status	stts	stop	stp

storage	strg /strj	structure	strctr
store	str	struggle	strgl
storm	strm	student	stdnt
story	st^y	studio	stdo
stove	stv	study	stdy
straight	strt	stuff	stf
straighten	strtn	stumble	stmbl
strain	strn /stran	stupid	stpd
strange	strng	stutter	sttr
stranger	stngr	style	styl
strangle	strgnl	stylish	styl$_s$
strapline	strpln	sub adolescence	^{s}adls^c
strategic	strtgc	sub adult	^{s}adlt
strategy	strtgy	subatomic	^{s}atmc
straw	strw	subcategory	^{s}ctg^y
strawberry	strwbry	subcommittee	^{sc}te
streak	strk	subconscious	^{sc}sos
stream	strm	subconsciousness	^{sc}sosns
street	strt / st	subcontinent	^{sc}tnnt
strength	strng$_t$	subcontract	^{sc}trct
strengthen	strng$_t$n	subcontractor	^{sc}trctr
stress	strs	subculture	^{s}cltr
stretch	str$_c$	subdivide	^{s}dvd
strict	strct	subdivision	^{s}dv^n
strictly	strct^y	subdue	^{s}du
strife	strf	subeditor	^{s}edtr
strike	strk	subgroup	^{s}grp
striking	strk^g	subheading	^{s}hd^g
string	str^g	subject	^{s}jct
stringent	strngnt	subjective	^{s}tjctv
strip	strp	sublease	^{s}les
strive	strv	sublet	^{s}lt
stroke	strk	sublevel	^{s}lvl
strong	strng	sublimate	^{s}lmt
strongly	strng^y	sublime	^{s}blim
structural	strctrl	subliminal	^{s}lmnl

submerge	^{s}mrg	subtlety	stlty
submission	^{s}m^n	subtly	st^y
submissive	^{s}tmsv	subtotal	^{s}ttl
submit	^{s}mt	subtract	^{s}trct / -
subnormal	^{s}nrml	subtraction	^{s}trc^n / -^{n}
subnormality	^{s}nrmlty	subtropical	^{s}trpcl
subordinate	^{s}ordnt	suburb	^{s}urb
subpoena	^{s}pena	suburban	^{s}urbn
subscribe	^{s}scrb	suburbia	^{s}rba
subscript	^{s}scrpt	subversion	^{s}vr^n
subsect	^{s}sct	subversive	^{s}vrsrv
subsequent	^{s}sqnt	subway	^{s}wy / ^{s}wa
subservient	^{s}srvint	succeed	scd
subset	^{s}st	success	scs
subside	^{s}sid	successful	scs^f
subsidence	^{s}sd^c	successfully	scs^{fy}
subsidiary	^{s}sdi^y	succession	scs^n
subsidise	^{s}sdis	such	s$_c$
subsidy	^{s}sdy	suck	sk
subsistence	^{s}sst^c	suction	sc^n
subsoil	^{s}sl	sudden	sdn
substance	^{s}stn^c	suddenly	sdn^y
substandard	^{s}stndrd	sue	su
substantial	^{s}stn^s	suffer	sfr
substantially	^{s}stn^{sy}	suffering	sfr^g
substantiate	^{s}stntt	sufficient	sfcnt
substantive	^{s}stntv	suffix	sfx
substation	^{s}st^n	suffocate	sfct
substitute	^{s}sttut	suffocation	sfc^n
substitution	^{s}stt^n	sugar	sgr
subsume	^{s}sum	suggest	sgst
subtext	^{s}txt	suggested	sgstd
subtitle	^{s}ttl	suggestion	sgs^n
subtitled	^{s}ttld	suicide	suicd
subtitles	^{s}ttls	suit	st
subtle	stl	suitable	st^b / sut^b

suite	sut	supernatural	^{s}ntrl
sum	sm	supernormal	^{s}nrml
summarise	smris	supernumerary	^{s}nm^y
summary	sm^y	superpose	^{s}imps
summer	smr	superscript	^{s}scrpt
summit	smt	supersede	^{s}cd
summon	smn	superseded	^{s}cdd
sun	sn	supersensitive	^{s}snstv
Sunday	su	superset	^{s}st
sundry	snd^y	supersize	^{s}sz
sunlight	snlt	superstar	^{s}str
sunny	sny	superstition	^{s}st^n
super	s	superstitious	^{s}stsos
superannuated	^{s}anutd	superstore	^{s}str
superb	^{s}b	supervise	^{s}vs
superbly	^{s}b^y	supervision	^{s}v^n
supercharger	^s_crgr	supervisor	^{s}vsr
supercilious	^{s}clios	supervisory	^{s}vs^y
superficial	sfs	supper	^{s}r
superficially	sfs^y	supple	^{s}l
superfine	^{s}fn	supplement	^{s}l^m
superfluous	^{s}flos	suppleness	^{s}lns
superglue	^{s}glu	supplicant	^{s}lcnt
superheavyweight	^{s}hvywt	supplied	^{s}ld
superhero	^{s}hro	supplier	^{s}lir
superheroine	^{s}hroin	supply	^{s}y
superhighway	^{s}hwy	support	^{s}rt
superhuman	^{s}hmn	supporter	^{s}rtr
superimpose	^{s}imps	supportive	^{s}rtv
superintelligent	^{s}intlgnt	suppose	^{s}ps
superintendent	^{s}intndnt	supposed	^{s}psd
superior	^{s}ir	supposedly	^{s}psd^y
superiority	^{s}irty	supposition	^{s}ps^n
superlative	^{s}ltv	suppress	^{s}prs
supermarket	^{s}mkt	suppression	^{s}pr^n
supermodel	^{s}mdl	supremacy	^{s}rmcy

supreme	ˢrem	sustenance	sstnᶜ
surcharge	sr_crᵍ	suture	sutr
surcharging	sr_crgᵍ	swab	swb
sure	sr / ₛr	swallow	swlw
surely	srʸ	swear	swr
surface	srfc	sweat	swt
surfeit	srft	sweater	swtr
surfing	srfᵍ	sweep	swp /swep
surgeon	srgen	sweet	swt /swet
surgery	srgʸ	swell	swl
surgical	srgcl	swerve	swrv
surmountable	srmntᵇ	swim	swm
surname	srnm	swimming	swmᵍ
surpass	srps	swindle	swndl
surplus	srpls	swing	swᵍ
surprise	srprs	switch	sw_c
surprised	srprsd	sword	swrd
surprising	srprsᵍ	sycamore	scmr
surprisingly	srprsᵍʸ	syllable	slᵇ
surrogate	srgt	symbol	smbl
surround	srnd	symbolic	smblc
surrounding	srndᵍ	symbolise	smblis
surveillance	srvlᶜ	sympathy	smp_ty
survey	srvy	symptom	smptm
surveyor	srvyr	syndicate	sndct
survival	srvvl	syndrome	sndrm
survive	srvv	syringe	srng / srnj
survivor	srvvr	system	sstm
susceptible	ssptᵇ		
suspect	sspct		
suspend	sspnd		
suspension	sspnⁿ		
suspicion	sspⁿ		
suspicious	sspcos		
sustain	sstn		
sustainable	sstnᵇ		

T

table	t[b]
tabled	t[b]d
tablespoon	t[b]spn / tbs
taboo	tbo
tabulated	tbultd / tab
tack	tk
tackle	tkl
tactful	tct[f]
tactic	tctc
tactical	tctcl
tadpole	tdpl
tag	tg
tagged	tgd
tail	tl
tailgating	tlgt[g]
tailor	tlr
take	tk
taken	tkn
taking	tk[g]
tale	tl / tal
talent	tlnt
talented	tlntd
talk	tlk
tall	tl
tangible	tng[b]
tangle	tngl
tank	tnk
tantalise	tntls
tantalising	tntls[g]
tap	tp
tape	tp / tap
taper	tpr
target	trgt
tariff	trf
tarnish	trn$_s$
task	tsk
taste	tst
tasteful	tst[f]
taunt	tnt
tax	tx
taxable	tx[b]
taxation	tx[n]
taxi	txi
taxpayer	txpyr
tea	t /te
teach	t$_c$
teacher	t$_c$r
teaching	t$_c$[g]
team	tm
teammate	tmmt
tear	tr
tearful	tr[f]
tease	ts
teaspoon	tspn
technical	t$_c$ncl
technician	t$_c$n[n]
technique	t$_c$nq
technological	t$_c$ol
technology	t$_c$o
teen	tn /ten
teenage	tng /tnj
teenager	tngr / tnjr
teetering	ttr[g]
teeth	t$_t$
teetotal	tettl
telecasting	tlecst[g]

108

teleconference	tl^{c}fr^c	terrible	tr^b
telephone	tlephn / tlefn / tel	terribly	tr^{by}
		terrific	trfc
telescope	tlscp	terrify	trfy
television	tlv^n / tv	territory	trt^y
tell	tl	terror	trr
temper	tmpr	terrorise	trrs
temperament	tmpr^m	terrorism	trrsm
temperamental	tmpr^{ml}	terrorist	trrst
temperature	tmprtr/ temp	tertiary	trt^y
template	tmplt	test	tst
temple	tmpl	testament	tst^m
temporary	tmpr^y	testify	tstfy
tempt	tmpt	testimony	tstmny
temptation	tmpt^n	testing	tst^g
tempted	tmptd	testosterone	tststrn
ten	10	tether	t$_t$r
tenancy	t^{c}y	text	txt
tenant	tnnt	textbook	txtbk
tend	tnd	textile	txtl
tendency	tnd^{cy}	texture	txtr
tender	tndr	than	$_t$n / tn
tendon	tndn	thank	$_t$nk
tennis	tns	thank you	tx / $_t$x / $_t$nk u
tense	t^c	thankful	$_t$nk^f
tension	tn^n	thankfully	$_t$nk^{fy}
tent	tnt	thanking	$_t$nk^g
tentative	tnttv	thanks	$_t$x / $_t$nks
tenth	10th / 10$_t$	Thanksgiving	$_t$xgv^g/$_t$nksgv^g
term	trm	that	$_t$t / tht
terminal	trmnl	that is	ie
terminate	trmnt	thatch	tc
termination	trmn^n	thaw	$_t$w
terms	trms	the	$_t$ / th / . / 7
terrace	trc	theatre	$_t$tr
terrain	trn /tran		

109

their	ₜr / thr	thoroughly	ₜrghʸ
them	ₜm / thm	those	ₜos / thos
theme	ₜem	though	ₜo
themself	ₜmslf	thought	ₜt
themselves	ₜmslvs	thoughtful	ₜtᶠ
then	ₜn / thn	thoughtfully	ₜtᶠʸ
theological	ₜol	thousand	1000
theology	ₜo	thread	ₜrd
theoretical	ₜrtcl	threat	ₜrt
theory	ₜʸ	threaten	ₜrtn
therapist	ₜrpst	three	3
therapy	ₜrpy	threshold	ₜrshld
there	ₜr / thr	thrift	ₜrft
thereby	ₜrby / thrby	thrive	ₜrv
therefore	∴	throat	ₜrt
thermal	ₜrml	thrombosis	ₜrmbss
these	ₜs / ths	throttle	ₜrtl
they	ₜy / thy	through	ₜru
thick	ₜk	throughout	ₜruot
thicken	ₜkn	throw	ₜrw
thief	ₜf	thrust	ₜrst
thieving	ₜvᵍ	Thursday	th
thigh	ₜi	thus	ₜs
thin	ₜn	thwarted	ₜwrtd
thing	ₜᵍ	thyroid	ₜrod
think	ₜnk	tick	tk
think tank	ₜnktnk	ticket	tkt
thinking	ₜnkᵍ	tickle	tkl
third	3rd / 1/3	tide	td
thirst	ₜrst	tidy	tdy
thirteen	13	tie	ti
thirty	30	tier	tr / ter
this	ₜi / thi	tiger	tgr
thorax	ₜrx	tight	tt
thorn	ₜrn	tighten	ttn
thorough	ₜrgh	tightly	ttʸ

tile	tl /til	ton	tn
till	tl	tone	tn / ton
tilt	tlt	tongue	tng
timber	tmbr	tonight	2nt
time	tm	tonne	tn /ton
time saver	tmsvr	too	2
time saving	tmsv^g	took	tk
timekeeping	tmkp^g	tool	tl
timetable	tmt^b	tooth	t$_t$
timing	tm^g	top	tp
tingle	tngl	topic	tpc
tinker	tnkr	Torah	trh
tinted	tntd	torment	tr^m
tiny	tny	torrential	trn^s
tip	tp	tortoise	trts /trtos
tire	tr	torture	trtr
tired	trd	toss	ts
tissue	tsu	total	ttl
titillating	ttlt^g	totalling	ttl^g
title	ttl	totally	tt^y
to	2	totter	ttr
toad	td /tod	touch	t$_c$
toast	tst	touchdown	t$_c$dn / t$_c$dwn
tobacco	tbco	tough	tgh / tf
today	2dy	tour	tr
toddler	tdlr	touring	tr^g
toe	to	tourism	trsm
together	tg$_t$r / 2g$_t$r	tourist	trst
toilet	tlt	tournament	trn^m
token	tkn	tow	tw
told	tld	toward	twrd /2wrd
tolerance	tlr^c	towards	twrds /2wrds
tolerate	tlrt	towel	twl
toll	tl	tower	twr
tomato	tmto	town	tn / twn
tomorrow	tmro / tom	toxic	txc

111

toy	ty	transform	^{t}frm
trace	trc / trs	transformation	^{t}frm^n
track	trk	transfusion	^{t}fu^n
traction	trc^n	transgender	^{t}gdr
trade	trd	transience	^{t}i^c
trading	trd^g	transient	^{t}ient
tradition	trd^n	transistor	^{t}istr
traditional	trd^{nl}	transit	^{t}t
traditionally	trd^{ny}	transition	^{t}i^n
traffic	trfc	translate	^{t}lt
tragedy	trgdy	translated	^{t}ltd
tragic	trgc	translation	^{t}l^n
trail	trl	translator	^{t}ltr
trailer	trlr	transmission	^{t}m^n
train	trn	transmit	^{t}mt
trainer	trnr	transmitter	^{t}mtr
training	trn^g	transparency	^{t}p^{cy}
trait	trt	transparent	^{t}prnt
trajectory	trjct^y	transpire	^{t}pr
trample	trmpl	transplant	^{t}plnt
trance	tr^c	transplantation	^{t}plnta^n
tranche	trn$_c$	transport	^{t}prt
transact	^{t}act	transportation	^{t}prta^n
transaction	^{t}act^n	transpose	^{t}ps
transactional	^{t}act^{nl}	transposed	^{t}psd
transcend	^{t}nd	transposes	^{t}pss
transcontinental	^{tc}tnntl	transposition	^{t}ps^n
transcribe	^{t}crb	transsexual	^{t}sxual / ^{t}
transcript	^{t}crpt	transverse	^{t}vrs
transcription	^{t}crp^n	transvestite	^{t}vstit
transfer	^{t}fr	trap	trp
transferable	^{t}fr^b	trash	tr$_s$
transfigure	^{t}fgr	trashing	tr$_s$^{g}
transfigured	^{t}fgrd	trauma	trma
transfix	^{t}fx	travel	trvl
transfixed	^{t}fxd		

112

traveller	trvlr	true	tru
traverse	trvrs	truly	tr^y
trawling	trwl^g	trumpet	trmpt
tray	try	truncate	trnct
treasure	trsr	truncated	trnctd
treat	trt	trunk	trnk
treatment	trt^m	trust	trst
treaty	trty	trustee	trste
treble	trbl / x3	trusteeship	trste^p
tree	tre	truth	tr$_t$
trek	trk	truthful	tr$_t^f$
tremble	trmbl	try	t^y
tremendous	trmndos	T-shirt	t-$_s$rt
trench	trn$_c$	tube	tub
trend	trnd	tuck	tk
trepidation	trpd^n	Tuesday	tu
trespass	trsps	tuft	tft
triage	trig / trij	tug	tg
trial	trl /tril	tuition	tui^n
triangle	trngl / Δ	tumble	tmbl
tribal	trbl	tumour	tmr
tribe	trb	tune	tun
tribulation	trbul^n	tunnel	tnl
trick	trk	turbulence	trbl^c
trigger	trgr	turbulent	trblnt
trim	trm	turf	trf
trip	trp	turkey	trky
triumph	trmf	turn	trn
troop	trp	turnover	trnovr
trophy	trphy / trfy	turtle	trtl
tropical	trpcl	tutor	ttr
trouble	trbl	tutorial	ttrl
troubled	trbld	TV	tv
truant	trunt	tweak	twk
truck	trk	tweet	twt
trudge	trg / trj	twelfth	12th / 12$_t$

113

twelve	12
twentieth	20th /20$_t$
twenty	20
twice	twc / x2
twin	twn
twinned	twnd
twist	twst
twitching	tw$_c$^{g}
twitter	twtr
two	2
two-thirds	2/3
type	typ
typecasting	typcst^g
typesetting	typst^g
typewriting	typrt^g
typical	tpcl
typically	tpc^y
typing	typ^g
tyranny	tyrny
tyre	tr

U

ugly	ug^y
uh	uh
ulcer	ulcr
ulceration	ulcr^n
ultimate	ultmt
ultimately	ultmt^y
ultimatum	ultmtm/ ultm
ultrasound	ultrsnd
umpire	umpr
unable	un^b
unappealing	unapel^g
unavailable	unavl^b
unavoidable	unavd^b
unbearable	unbr^b
unbeatable	unbt^b
unbreakable	unbrk^b
uncaring	uncr^g
uncertain	uncrtn
uncertainty	uncrtnty
unchanging	un$_c$ng^g
uncle	uncl
uncomfortable	un^{c}4t^b
uncouth	unc$_t$
uncover	uncvr
undecided	undcdd
undemanding	undmnd^g
undeniable	undni^b
under	u
underachieve	^{u}a$_c$v
underachievement	^{u}a$_c$v^m
underactive	^{u}actv

114

underactivity	ᵘactvty	underpowered	ᵘpwrd
underarm	ᵘarm	underprepared	ᵘᵖprd
underbelly	ᵘbʸ	underpriced	ᵘpricd
underbid	ᵘbd	underprivileged	ᵘprvlgd
undercarriage	ᵘcrg / ᵘcrj	underrate	ᵘrt
undercharge	ᵘ_cg	underrated	ᵘrtd
underclass	ᵘcls	underreported	ᵘrprtd
underclothes	ᵘcl_ts	underscore	ᵘscr
undercoat	ᵘct	underscored	ᵘscrd
undercut	ᵘct	undersell	ᵘsl
underdeveloped	ᵘdvlpd / ᵘdev	underside	ᵘsd
underdog	ᵘdg	undersize	ᵘsz
undereducated	ᵘedctd	understaffed	ᵘstfd
underemployed	ᵘemplyd	understand	ᵘstnd
underestimate	ᵘestmt	understandable	ᵘstndᵇ
underestimation	ᵘestmⁿ	understandably	ᵘstndᵇʸ
underexpose	ᵘxps	understanding	ᵘstndᵍ
underfed	ᵘfd	understate	ᵘstt
undergo	ᵘgo	understated	ᵘsttd
undergoing	ᵘgᵍ	understatement	ᵘsttᵐ
undergraduate	ᵘgrdut/ ᵘgrd	understood	ᵘstd
underground	ᵘgrnd	understrength	ᵘstrng_t
undergrowth	ᵘgrw_t	understudy	ᵘstdy
underhand	ᵘhnd	undertake	ᵘtk
underinvestment	ᵘinvstᵐ	undertaken	ᵘtkn
underlay	ᵘly	undertaker	ᵘtkr
underline	ᵘln	undertone	ᵘtn
underlined	ᵘlnd	undertook	ᵘtk
underlying	ᵘlyᵍ	underused	ᵘusd
undermine	ᵘmn	underutilise	ᵘtls
underneath	ᵘn_t	undervaluation	ᵘvluⁿ
underpaid	ᵘpd	undervalue	ᵘvlu
underpay	ᵘpy / ᵘpa	underwater	ᵘwtr
underpayment	ᵘpᵐ	underway	ᵘwy
underpin	ᵘpn	underweight	ᵘwt
underpinned	ᵘpnd	underwent	ᵘwnt

underwrite	ᵘrt	universal	unvrsl
underwritten	ᵘrtn	universe	unvrs
undeserving	unᵈrvᵍ	university	unvsty / uni
undesirable	unᵈrᵇ	unknowing	unnwᵍ
undisclosed	unᵈclsd	unknown	unnwn
undoing	undᵍ	unlawful	unlwᶠ
uneasy	unesy	unleash	unlₛ
uneconomic	uneco	unless	unls
uneducated	unedctd	unlikable	unlkᵇ
unemployed	unempld	unlike	unlk
unemployment	unemplᵐ	unlikely	unlkʸ
unenviable	unenvᵇ	unload	unld
unethical	uneₜcl	unlock	unlk
uneventful	unevntᶠ	unmanageable	unmnjᵇ / unmngᵇ
unexpected	unxpctd		
unfair	unfr	unnerve	unnrv
unfaithful	unfₜᶠ	unofficial	unofˢ
unfavourable	unfvrᵇ	unopposed	unopsd
unfold	unfld	unpack	unpck
unfortunately	unᶠtntʸ / un4tntʸ	unprecedented	unᵖcdntd
		unprintable	unprntᵇ
ungrateful	ungrtᶠ	unreachable	unrᴄᵇ
unhappy	unhpy	unreadable	unrdᵇ
unhelpful	unhlpᶠ	unreasonable	unrsnᵇ
unification	unifcⁿ	unreliable	unrlᵇ
uniform	unfrm	unsettling	unstlᵍ
uninsurable	uninsrᵇ	unsociable	unscᵇ
unintentionally	unintnⁿʸ	unsocial	unsˢ
union	unn	unspeakable	unspkᵇ
unique	unq	unstable	unstᵇ
unit	unt	unstoppable	unstpᵇ
unite	unt /unit	unsuitable	unstᵇ
United	untd /utd	untenable	untnᵇ
uniting	untᵍ	unthinkable	unₜnkᵇ
unity	unty		

unthinking	un_tnk^g	utilise	utils
untidy	untdy	utility	utlty
until	untl	utterance	utr^c
untouchable	unt_c^b		
untraceable	untrc^b		
unusable	unus^b		
unusual	unusl		
unutterable	unutr^b		
unwavering	unwvr^g		
unwitting	unwt^g		
unworkable	unwrk^b		
up	up		
upcoming	upcm^g		
update	updt		
upgrade	upgrd		
uplifting	uplft^g		
upmarket	upmrkt		
upon	upn		
upper	upr		
uprising	uprs^g		
upset	upst		
upshot	up_st		
upstage	upstg / upstj		
upstairs	upstrs		
urban	urbn		
urchin	ur_cn		
urge	urg		
us	us		
usable	us^b		
use	us		
used	usd		
useful	us^f		
user	usr		
using	us^g		
usual	usl		
usually	us^y		

117

V

vacancy	vcncy / vac	vengeance	vng[c]
vacation	vc[n]	ventilate	vntlt
vaccination	vcn[n]	ventilation	vntl[n]
vaccine	vcin	venture	vntr
vacuum	vcm	verb	vrb
valid	vld	verbal	vrbl
validate	vldt	verbatim	vrbtm
validation	vld[n]	verdict	vrdct
validity	vldty	verge	vrg / vrj
valley	vly	verging	vrg[g]
valuable	vlu[b] / vl[b]	verifiable	vrfi[b]
valuation	vlu[n]	verified	vrfd
value	vlu	verify	vrf
van	vn	verse	vrs
vanish	vn[s]	version	vs[n]
vaporise	vprs	versus	vrss /vs
variable	vri[b]	vertebra	vrtba
variance	vri[c]	vertical	vrtcl
variation	vri[n]	very	v
variety	vrty	vessel	vsl
various	vros	veteran	vtrn
varnish	vrn[s]	veto	vto
vary	v[y]	via	va
vascular	vsclr	viable	vi[b]
vast	vst	vibrant	vbrnt
vegetable	vgt[b] / veg	vibrate	vbrt
vegetation	vgt[n]	vibration	vbr[n]
vehicle	vhcl	vicar	vcr
vending	vnd[g]	victim	vctm
vendor	vndr	victimise	vctmis
venerable	vnr[b]	victorious	victros
		victory	vct[y]
		video	vdo
		video conference	vdo [c]fr[c]
		view	vw
		viewer	vwr

vigilance	vgl[c]	vowel	vwl
vigilant	vglnt	voyage	vyg / vyj
village	vlj / vlg	vs	vs
violate	vlt	vulgar	vlgr
violation	vl[n]	vulnerable	vlnr[b]
violence	vl[c]		
violent	vlnt		
viral	vrl		
virtual	vrtl		
virtually	vrt[y]		
virtue	vrtu		
virus	vrs		
visible	vs[b]		
vision	v[n]		
visit	vst		
visitor	vstr		
visual	vsl /visul		
vital	vtl		
vivisection	vvsc[n]		
vocabulary	vcbl[y] / vocab / vcb		
vocal	vcl		
vocalise	vclis		
vocals	vcls		
vocation	vc[n]		
voice	vc		
void	vd		
volume	vlm /vol		
voluntary	vlnt[y]		
volunteer	vlntr		
vomit	vmt		
vote	vt		
voter	vtr		
voting	vt[g]		
vouch	v$_c$		
voucher	v$_c$r		

119

W

wage	wj / wg
waged	wjd / wgd
wagon	wgn
waist	wst
wait	wt
wake	wk
Wales	wls
walk	wlk
walking	wlk^g
wall	wl
wander	wndr /wandr
want	wnt
war	wr
warehouse	wrhs
warm	wrm
warmth	wrm$_t$
warn	wrn
warning	wrn^g
warpath	wrp$_t$
warrant	wrnt
warranty	wrnty
warrior	wrr
warship	wr^p
was	ws
wash	w$_s$
wasp	wsp
wastage	wstj / wstg
waste	wst
wasteful	wst^f
watch	w$_c$
watchdog	w$_c$dg
watchful	w$_c^f$
water	wtr / h2o
wave	wv
way	wy
we	w
weak	wk
weaken	wkn
weakness	wkns
wealth	wl$_t$
wealthy	wl$_t$y
weapon	wpn
wear	wr
wearable	wr^b
weather	w$_t$r
weave	wv /wev
web	wb
webcast	wbcst
wedding	wd^g
Wednesday	we
weed	wd
week	wk
weekday	wkdy
weekend	wknd
weekly	wk^y
weigh	wgh
weight	wt
weird	wrd
welcome	wlcm
welfare	wlfr
well	wl
well-being	wl-b
well-known	w-nwn
went	wnt
were	wr
west	wst / w
western	wstrn

wet	wt	wife	wf
whale	$_w$l	wild	wld
what	wh / $_w$	wilderness	wldrns
whatever	$_w$evr	wildlife	wldlf
wheat	$_w$t	will	wl
wheel	$_w$l / $_w$el	willing	wl^g
wheelchair	$_w$l$_c$r	willingness	wl^{g}ns
when	whn / $_w$n	win	wn
whenever	$_w$nevr	winch	wn$_c$
where	whr / $_w$r	wind	wnd
whereas	$_w$ras	window	wndo
wherever	$_w$revr	windpipe	wndpp
whether	$_{wt}$r	wine	wn /win
which	wc	wing	w^g
while	whl / $_w$l	winner	wnr
whip	$_w$p	winter	wntr
whisky	$_w$sky	wipe	wp
whisper	$_w$spr	wire	wr
whistle	$_w$stl	wireless	wrls
white	$_w$t	wisdom	wsdm
who	$_w$o	wise	ws
whoever	$_w$oevr	wish	w$_s$
whole	$_w$l	wishful	w$_s$f
wholesale	$_w$lsl	wistful	wst^f
whom	$_w$m	with	wi / w$_t$
whose	$_w$s	withdraw	w$_t$drw
why	y	withdrawal	w$_t$drwl
wide	wd	withhold	w$_t$hld
widely	wd^y	within	w/i w/ n
widespread	wdsprd	without	w/o w/ou
widow	wdo	witness	wtns
width	wd$_t$	wives	wvs
wield	wld	wolf	wlf
		woman	wmn
		women	wmn / wmen
		won't	wnt

121

XYZ

wonder	wndr		
wonderful	wndr^f		
wood	wd		
wooden	wdn		
word	wrd	x-rated	xrtd
work	wrk	x-ray	xry
workable	wrk^b		
worker	wrkr	yard	yrd
workforce	wrkfrc	yeah	yh
working	wrk^g	year	yr
workmanship	wrkmn^p	yell	yl
workout	wrkot	yellow	ylw
workplace	wrkplc	yes	ys / y / ✓
works	wrks	yesterday	ystrdy
workshop	wrk$_s$p	yet	yt
workstation	wrkst^n	yield	yld
world	wrld	you	u
worldwide	wrldwd	young	yng
worried	wrd	youngster	yngstr
worry	w$^{y.}$	your	ur
worse	wrs	yours	urs
worsen	wrsn	yourself	urslf
worship	wr^p	youth	y$_t$
worth	wr$_t$	youthful	y$_t^f$
would	wd	youthfully	y$_t^{fy}$
wound	wnd		
wow	wo	zeal	zl
wrap	wrp / rp	zebra	zbr
wrist	wrst /rst	zen	zn
write	rt	zenith	zn$_t$
writer	rtr	zone	zn
writing	rt^g	zoo	zo
written	rtn	zoological	z^{o}cl
wrong	rng	zoology	z^o
wrong doing	rngd^g		
wrote	wrt / wrot		

**Speed Writing
Modern Shorthand
An Easy to Learn
Note Taking System
UK Spelling Version**

**Heather Baker
ISBN: 978-1537566603**

Learn a new hand writing system in a matter of hours and become really quick in just a few weeks.

* This book is laid out in easy to follow lessons
* Practical guided exercises, with example answers
* Save time and become efficient at taking dictation, in meetings, on the telephone and in lectures
* No strange squiggles to learn – just different ways to use the letters you already know
* Your notes will be easy to read and transcribe
* Adapt the system to suit your needs

A terrific opportunity to save time and become more efficient.

"I am thoroughly enjoying learning a new skill from a book that is so simple to understand and I have already started to implement it."

"I will use this system all the time."

"This is so easy to learn and use."

Printed in Great Britain
by Amazon